'FOREIGN TRADE DEVELOPMENT AND REGULATION ACT'- SUPREME COURT AND HIGH COURT'S LEADING CASE LAWS

CASE NOTES- FACTS- FINDINGS OF APEX COURT JUDGES & CITATIONS

JAYPRAKASH BANSILAL SOMANI

All the Past & Present Judges of the Supreme Court of India.

Salute to their wisdom.

Salute to their interpretation of Law.

Salute to their elaborative judgement writing.

Supreme Court of India.

Contents

Contents

Preface

Dear Learned Advocates of CESTAT, Trial Court, High court and Supreme Court, Corporate and Individuals.

I am very delighted to provide you a book on 'FOREIGN TRADE DEVELOPMENT AND REGULATION ACT'- SUPREME COURT'S LATEST LEADING CASE LAWs

In this book you will get...

1. Name of the Case i. e. Cause title

2.Relevant Sections discussed in the case

3. Hon'ble Judges/Coram of the case

4.Number of PDF Pages in Original Judgement of the case

5. All available Citations of the case

6. Case Note with appeal allowed/ dismissed or disposed off

7. Facts of the case

8. Hon'ble Apex Court's findings, while dismissing/allowing or disposing the appeal

9. Ratio Decidendi if any.

My special thanks to Manupatra, because of their web portal I can compile this book in well manner. I am also thankful to Notion Press to support me to publish & market this book throughout the Country. Thanks to my Juniors, Advocate Colleagues & Insolvency Professional Colleagues to support me in this venture.

Adv. Manoj Kumar Chowdhary & Miss. Pooja Rai has helped me a lot to compile this book. I hope this book will add some value addition in the wealth of your legal knowledge. Your positive feedbacks will boost me to compile/ write further books & negative feedbacks will improve my skills. Kindly send your valuable feedbacks by email.

Thanks with Regards,

Jayprakash B. Somani

Advocate, Supreme Court of India

Email: jaysomani64@gmail.com

Web Site:www.jayprakashsomani.com

Call: 9322188701, 8459194576

Acknowledgements

Printed & Published by
Notion Press
No. 8, 3rd Cross Street,
CIT Colony, Mylapore,
Chennai, Tamil Nadu- 600004
Managed by
Jayprakash Somani Advocates & Solicitors
Law Firm for Supreme Court of India
Delhi Office
B- 851, 1st Floor, Shivaji Marg, New Ashok Nagar, Delhi 110096.
Call: 9322188701, 8459194576
Supreme Court Chamber
312, 3rd Floor, M. C. Setalvad Block, In front of 'D' Gate, Bhagwan Das Road, Supreme Court of India, New Delhi 110001
Contact: 8459194576, 9811011747
www.jayprakashsomani.com
Download our app to get access to our Free Videos, Free Bare Acts, Free Study Material in Legal as well as International Business Regime.
Android App Link ;-https://clpandrea.page.link/cmSm
Ios APp Link :-https://apps.apple.com/us/app/classplus/id1324522260
Login with org code ;- (qywzji)
Web Link ;-https://qywzji.courses.store/
Opportunity for Lawyers/ Social Workers to get Supreme Court Law Firm JSAS's authorised centre at District Level.
Kindly Message or Call to: 9322188701
Books are available online in India
1.Notion Press:https://notionpress.com/author/jayprakash_somani
2.Amazon:https://www.amazon.in/s?k=jayprakash+somani
3.Flipkart:https://www.flipkart.com/search?q=Jayprakash%20Somani
Books are available online at International Market
4. **Amazon International:** https://www.amazon.com/s?k=jayprakash+somani
5. **Amazon United Kingdom:** https://www.amazon.co.uk/s?k=jayprakash+somani

6. **E-Books/Kindle edition at National & International Level:** https://www.amazon.in/s?k=jaypraksh+somani

Moser Baer Karamchari Union thr. President Mahesh Chand Sharma vs. Union of India (UOI) and Ors. (02.05.2023 – SC) : MANU/SC/0507/2023

Relative Section:

Companies Act, 1956 - Section 529, Section 529A, Section 529(1), Section 529(3),Section 530, Section 530(1); Section 271, Section 272, Section 324, Section 325, Section 325(1), Section 326, Section 326(1),Section 326(2), Section 327, Section 327(7); Constitution of India - Article 14, Article 21, Article 32; Employee's Compensation Act, 1923 - Section 14; Industrial Disputes Act, 1947 - Section 2, Section 2(s); Insolvency And Bankruptcy Code, 2016 - Section 5, Section 5(16), Section 29A, Section 30,Section 31,Section 33, Section 34, Section 35, Section 36,Section 36(4), Section 37 to Section53, Section 53(1),Insolvency And Bankruptcy Code, 2016 - Section 54, Insolvency And Bankruptcy Code, 2016 - Section 61 to Section 62, Insolvency And Bankruptcy Code, 2016 - Section 255

Hon'bleJudges/Coram:

M.R. Shah and Sanjiv Khanna, JJ.

Equivalent Citation: III(2023)BC237(SC), [2023]238CompCas458(SC), 2023/INSC/479

Case Reference:

Manish Kumar v. Union of India (UOI) and Ors. MANU/SC/0029/2021; Swiss Ribbons Pvt. Ltd. and Ors. v. Union of India (UOI) and Ors. MANU/SC/0079/2019; Small Scale Industrial Manufactures Association (Regd.) v. Union of India (UOI) and Ors. MANU/SC/0202/2021; Committee of Creditors of Essar Steel India Limited v. Satish Kumar Gupta and Ors. MANU/SC/1577/2019; Ghanashyam Mishra and Sons Private Limited v. Edelweiss Asset Reconstruction Company Limited and Ors. MANU/SC/0273/2021; Allahabad Bank v. Canara Bank and Ors. MANU/SC/0262/2000; Andhra Bank v. Official Liquidator and Ors. MANU/SC/0203/2005; Innoventive Industries Ltd. v. ICICI Bank and Ors. MANU/SC/1063/2017; ArcelorMittal India Private Limited v. Satish Kumar Gupta and Ors. MANU/SC/1123/2018; Arun Kumar Jagatramka v. Jindal Steel and Power Ltd. and Ors. MANU/SC/0182/2021; Sesh Nath Singh and Ors. v. Baidyabati Sheoraphuli Co-operative Bank Ltd. and Ors. MANU/SC/0205/2021; R.K. Garg and Ors. v. Union of India (UOI) and Ors. MANU/SC/0074/1981; Rustom Cavasjee Cooper and Ors. v. Union of India (UOI) MANU/SC/0011/1970; Delhi Science Forum and Ors. v. Union of India (UOI) and Ors. MANU/SC/0360/1996; BALCO Employees Union v. Union of India (UOI) and Ors. MANU/SC/0779/2001; Bhavesh D. Parish and Ors. v. Union of India (UOI) and Ors. MANU/SC/0392/2000; Director General of Foreign Trade and Ors. v. Kanak Exports and Ors. MANU/SC/1258/2015; Employees Provident Fund Commissioner v. O.L. of Esskay Pharmaceuticals Limited MANU/SC/1327/2011; Bhupinder Singh v. Unitech Limited, MANU/SCOR/47410/2020

NumberofPagesintheOriginalJudgment:32

Case Note:

Company -Liquidation - Workmen dues - Sections 271, 326, 327 and 327(7) of Companies Act, 2013, Sections 36(4), 52, 53, 53(1)(b) of Insolvency and Bankruptcy Code, 2016, Regulation 21A of Insolvency and Bankruptcy Board of India Regulations, 2016and Articles 14 and 21 of Constitution of India- Present petition filed for striking down Section 327(7) of Act, 2013 as arbitrary and violative of Article 21 of Constitution of India-Petitioner had also sought for appropriate direction so as to leave statutory claims of workmen's dues out of purview of waterfall mechanism under Section 53 of Code, 2016 - Whether Section 327(7) of Act, 2013 which states that 326 and 327 of Act, 2013 shall not be applicable in event of liquidation under IBC could be said to be arbitrary and/or violative of Article 21 of Constitution of India.

Facts:

By way of this writ petition, Petitioner had prayed for an appropriate writ, direction or order striking down Section 327(7) of the Companies Act, 2013 as arbitrary and violative of Article 21 of the Constitution of India. It was also prayed to issue an appropriate writ, direction or order in the nature of Mandamus so as to leave the statutory claims of the workmen's dues out of the purview of waterfall mechanism under Section 53 of the Insolvency and Bankruptcy Code, 2016.

Held, while dismissing the petition:

(i) The Companies Act, 2013 did not deal with insolvency and bankruptcy when the companies are unable to pay their debts or the aspects relating to the revival and rehabilitation of the companies and their winding up if revival and rehabilitation is not possible. In principle, it could not be doubted that the cases of revival or winding up of the company on the ground of insolvency and inability to pay debts are different from cases where companies were wound up under Section 271 of the Companies Act 2013. The two situations were not identical. under Section 271 of the Companies Act, 2013, even a running and financially sound company can also be wound up for the reasons in Clauses (a) to (e). The reasons and grounds for winding up under Section 271 of the Companies Act, 2013 were vastly different from the reasons and grounds for the revival and rehabilitation scheme as envisaged under the Code. The two enactments deal with two distinct situations andthey could not be equated when we examine whether there was discrimination or violation of Article 14 of the Constitution of India. For the revival and rehabilitation of the companies, certain sacrifices were required from all quarters, including the workmen. In case of insolvent companies, for the sake of survival and regeneration, everyone, including the secured creditors and the Central and State Government, were required to make sacrifices. The workmen also have a stake and benefit from the revival of the company, and therefore unless it was found that the sacrifices envisaged for the workmen, which certainly form a separate class, were onerous and burdensome so as to be manifestly unjust and arbitrary, this court would not set aside the legislation, solely on the ground that some or marginal sacrifice is to be made by the workers. This court would also reject the argument that to find out whether there was a violation of Article 14 of the Constitution of India or whether the right to life under Article 21 Constitution of India was infringed, this court must word by word examine the waterfall mechanism envisaged under the Companies Act, 2013, where the company was wound up in terms of grounds (a) to (e) of Section 271 of the Companies Act, 2013 and the rights of the workmen when the insolvent company was sought to be revived, rehabilitated or wound up under the Code. The grounds and situations in the context of the objective and purpose of the two enactments were entirely different. [9]

(ii) To protect the interest of the workmen where the secured creditor did not relinquish its security interest to fall under Section 53 of the Code, Regulation 21A of the Insolvency and Bankruptcy Board of India (Liquidation Process) Regulations, 2016 had been enacted, and it requires that the secured creditor, who opts to realise its security interest as per Section 52 of the Code, had to pay as much towards the amount payable under the Clause (a) and Sub-clause (i) to Clause (b) of Sub-section (1) to Section 53 of the Code to the liquidator within the time and the manner stipulated therein. The workmen's dues, even when the secured creditor opts to proceed under Section 52 of the Code, are therefore protected in terms of Sub-clause (b) of Sub-section (1) to Section 53 of the Code. [13]

(iii) The Code is based on the organic evolution of law and is a product of an extensive consultative process to meet the requirements of the Code governing liquidation. It introduced a comprehensive and time-bound framework to maximise the value of assets of all persons and balance the interest of the stakeholders. The guiding principle for the Code in setting the priority of payments in liquidation was to bring the practices in India in line with global practices. In the waterfall mechanism, after the costs of the insolvency resolution process and liquidation, secured creditors share the highest priority along with a defined period of dues of the workmen. The unpaid dues of the workmen are adequately and significantly protected in line with the objectives sought to be achieved by the Code and in terms of the waterfall mechanism prescribed by Section 53 of the Code. In either case of relinquishment or non-relinquishment of the security by the secured creditor, the interests of workmen are protected under the Code. In fact, the secured creditors were taking significant hair-cut and workmen were being compensated on an equitable basis in a just and proper manner as per Section 53 of the Code. The Code balances the rights of the secured creditors, who are financial institutions in which the general public had invested money, and also ensures that the economic activity and revival of a viable company is not hindered because it has suffered or fallen into a financial crisis. The Code focuses on bringing additional gains to both the economy and the exchequer through efficiency enhancement and consequent greater value capture. In economic matters, a wider latitude is given to the law- maker and the Court allows for experimentation in such legislations based on practical experiences and other problems seen by the law-makers. In a challenge to such legislation, the Court does not adopt a doctrinaire approach. Some sacrifices have to be always made for the greater good, and unless such sacrifices are prima facie apparent and ex facie harsh and unequitable as to classify as manifestly arbitrary, these would be interfered with by the court. [17]

(iv) As Sub-section (7) of Section 327 of the Act, 2013 provides that Sections 326 and 327 of the Act, 2013 shall not be applicable in the event of liquidation under the IBC, which had been necessitated in view of the enactment of IBC and it applies with respect to the liquidation of a company under the IBC, Section 327(7) of the Act, 2013 could not be said to be arbitrary and/or violative of Article 21 of the Constitution of India. In case of the liquidation of a company under the IBC, the distribution of the assets shall have to be made as per Section 53 of the IBC subject to Section 36(4) of the IBC, in case of liquidation of company under IBC. [18]

CHAPTER TWO

Akshay N. Patel vs. Reserve Bank of India and Ors. (06.12.2021 - SC) : MANU/SC/1187/2021

Relative Section:

Constitution of India - Article 14, Article 19, Article 19(1) to Article 19(6), Article 15, Article 16, Article 17, Article 20, Article 21,Article 22(1), Article 23 to Article 28,Constitution of India - Article 29(1), Article 30(1), Article 31(1), Article 31(2), Article 32, Article 47, Article 226, Article 372(1); Aadhaar (Targeted Delivery of Financial and other Subsidies, benefits and services) Act, 2016; Banking Regulation Act, 1949; Disaster Management Act, 2005; Foreign Exchange Management Act, 1999 - Section 10(1), Section 11(1),Section 3,Section 10(4); Foreign Trade (Development & Regulation) Act, 1992 - Section 3, Section 3(2); Reserve Bank of India Act, 1934 - Section 3(1),Section 20,Section 21(1),Section 22(1), Section 45Z,Section 38

Hon'bleJudges/Coram:

Dr. D.Y. Chandrachud, Vikram Nath and B.V. Nagarathna, JJ.

Equivalent Citation: 2022(379)ELT3(S.C.), (2022)3SCC694, [2021]13SCR231

Case Reference:

Shri Sitaram Sugar Co. Ltd. and Ors. v. Union of India (UOI) and Ors. MANU/SC/0249/1990; Prag Ice and Oil Mills and Ors. v. Union of India (UOI) MANU/SC/0493/1978; P.T.R. Exports (Madras) Pvt. Ltd. and Ors. v. Union of India (UOI) and Ors. MANU/SC/0943/1996; The State Trading

Corporation of India Ltd. and Ors. v. The Commercial Tax Officer, Visakhapatnam and Ors. MANU/SC/0038/1963; Chintaman Rao and Ors. v. State of Madhya Pradesh MANU/SC/0008/1950; M.R.F. Ltd. v. Inspector Kerala Govt. and Ors. MANU/SC/0702/1998; The State of Uttar Pradesh v. Kaushaliya and Ors. MANU/SC/0091/1963; Kavalappara Kottarathil Kochuni and Ors. v. The State of Madras and Ors. MANU/SC/0019/1960; O.K. Ghosh and Ors. v. E.X. Joseph MANU/SC/0362/1962; B.P. Sharma v. Union of India (UOI) and Ors. MANU/SC/0598/2003; Saghir Ahmad v. The State of U.P. and Ors. MANU/SC/0110/1954; J.K. Industries Ltd. and Ors. v. Chief Inspector of Factories and Boilers and Ors. MANU/SC/1293/1996; Justice K.S. Puttaswamy and Ors. v. Union of India (UOI) and Ors. MANU/SC/1044/2017; Om Kumar and Ors. v. Union of India (UOI) MANU/SC/0704/2000; Modern Dental College and Research Centre and Ors. v. State of Madhya Pradesh and Ors. MANU/SC/0495/2016; Rustom Cavasjee Cooper and Ors. v. Union of India (UOI) MANU/SC/0011/1970; Shayara Bano and Ors. v. Union of India (UOI) and Ors. MANU/SC/1031/2017; A.K. Gopalan v. The State of Madras MANU/SC/0012/1950; Maneka Gandhi v. Union of India (UOI) and Ors. MANU/SC/0133/1978; State of Andhra Pradesh and Ors. v. McDowell and Co. and Ors. MANU/SC/0427/1996; Joseph Kuruvilla Vellukunnel v. The Reserve Bank of India and Ors. MANU/SC/0057/1962; Peerless General Finance and Investment Co. Limited and Ors. v. Reserve Bank of India and Ors. MANU/SC/0685/1992; Internet and Mobile Association of India v. Reserve Bank of India MANU/SC/0264/2020; R.K. Garg and Ors. v. Union of India (UOI) and Ors. MANU/SC/0074/1981; BALCO Employees Union v. Union of India (UOI) and Ors. MANU/SC/0779/2001; Swiss Ribbons Pvt. Ltd. and Ors. v. Union of India (UOI) and Ors. MANU/SC/0079/2019; Dwarka Prasad Laxmi Narain v. The State of Uttar Pradesh and Ors. MANU/SC/0030/1954; Shree Meenakshi Mills Ltd. and Ors. v. Union of India (UOI) MANU/SC/0064/1973; Indian Handicrafts Emporium and Ors. v. Union of India (UOI) and Ors. MANU/SC/0640/2003; Narendra Kumar and Ors. v. The Union of India (UOI) and Ors. MANU/SC/0013/1959; Mohammed Faruk v. State of Madhya Pradesh and Ors. MANU/SC/0046/1969; Cellular Operators Association of India and Ors. v. Telecom Regulatory Authority of India and Ors. MANU/SC/0551/2016; Sukhnandan Saran Dinesh Kumar and Ors. v. Union of India (UOI) and Ors. MANU/SC/0020/1982; Ebix Singapore v. Committee of Creditors of Educomp Solutions (P) Ltd.; R. v. Oakes MANU/SCCN/0042/1986 : (1986) 1 SCR 103; Jalan Trading Co. v.

D.M. Aney AIR 1973 SC 233; Aparna Chandra, "Proportionality in India: A Bridge to Nowhere" (2020) 3(2) University of Oxford Human Rights Hub Journal 55; Alec Stone Sweet and Jud Mathews, "Proportionality Balancing and Global Constitutionalism" (2008-2009) 47 Columbia Journal of Transnational Law 72; Vicki C Jackson, "Constitutional Law in an Age of Proportionality" (2015) 124(8) Yale Law Journal 3094; Laxmi Khandsari v. State of Uttar Pradesh MANU/SC/0067/1981 : AIR 1981 SC 860

NumberofPagesintheOriginalJudgment: 31

Case Note:

Constitution - Ban of PPE products from import/ export - Validity of Policy guideline - Infringement of fundamental rights - Constitutionality of Clause 2(iii) of the Merchanting Trade Transactions (MTT) Guidelines, 2020questioned - Provision alleged to be violating rights guaranteed under Articles 14, 19(1)(g) and 21 of the Constitution of India, 1950 - High Court by impugned judgment upheld Clause 2(iii) of the Revised Guidelines - Whether restriction to prohibit MTTs in PPE products restrictive of rights to equality, freedom to conduct trade, liberty and right to livelihood?

Facts:

Appellant obtained international MTT contract to serve as an intermediary between the sale of PPE products by a supplier in China to a buyer in the United States. Requisite permission sought was denied by RBI on the basis of clause 2(iii) of the 2020 MTT Guidelines as at the relevant time, export of PPE products was banned by relevant notifications due to the ongoing COVID-19 pandemic.Appellant filed a writ petition contending clause 2(iii) of the 2020 MTT Guidelines as unconstitutional since it violated Appellant's right to carry on business under Article 19(1)(g) and the right to life and livelihood under Article 21 of the Constitution. The petition was dismissed on the premise that clause 2(iii) only prohibited MTTs for goods that cannot be imported/exported into India. The provision is general in its application and does not specifically prohibit MTT in PPE products. Further decision to modify the FTP to prohibit import/export of goods is a policy decision. Hence, the present appeal.

Held, while dismissing the Appeal:

Ban on exports, imports and MTTs of PPE products is to ensure the availability of adequate domestic supplies during a global health pandemic. Adequate stocks of PPE products are critical for the healthcare system to combat the COVID-19 pandemic. The State's aim of ensuring supplies is in furtherance of the right to life under Article 21 and the Directive Principles of State Policy mandating the State's improvement of public health as a primary duty Under Article 47. The Appellant has not challenged the legitimacy of this aim of ensuring adequate PPE in India. The executive's aim to ensure sufficient availability of PPE products, considering the ongoing pandemic, is legitimate. Accordingly, the impugned measure is enacted in furtherance of a legitimate aim that is of sufficient importance to override a constitutional right of freedom to conduct business.[29]

While the goods involved in an MTT never enter the territory of the intermediary, they are still recorded as negative and positive exports from the territory of intermediary during the import and export leg of the MTT, which is similar to how ordinary imports and exports would be recorded.[42]

It was suitable for the RBI to link the permissibility of MTT in goods to the permissibility of their import/export under the FTP. Appellant has not challenged notifications prohibiting the export of PPE products under the FTP. Hence, the prohibition of their MTT under Clause 2(iii) of the 2020 MTT Guidelines is also considered suitable.[44]

Appellant's arguments rejected for two reasons. First, while MTTs in PPE products may not directly reduce the stock of these products in India, it still does contribute to their trade between two foreign nations. In doing so, it directly reduces the available quantity of PPE products in the international market, which may have been bought by India, if so required. As such, MTTs contribute to reducing the available stock of PPE products in the international market that India could have acquired. Second, the UOI's policy to ban the export of PPE products reflects their stance on the product's non-tradability during the COVID-19 pandemic. It highlights a clear policy choice under which Indian entities shall not be allowed to export these products outside of India, in all probability to the highest buyers across the globe who may end up hoarding the global supply. Hence, banning MTTs in PPE products was critical in ensuring that Indian foreign exchange reserves are not utilized to facilitate the hoarding of PPE products with wealthier nations. A mere ban on exports would not regulate the utilisation of Indian foreign exchange. Hence, in order to keep India's policy position consistent across the board, the prohibition of MTTs in respect of PPE products was necessary and the only alternative of ensuring the realisation of legitimate State interest.[47]

RBI is a special, expert regulatory body that is insulated from the political arena. Its decisions are reflective of its expertise in guiding the economic policy and financial stability of the nation.[54]

Judgment of the High Court was correct in holding that Clause 2(iii) of the 2020 MTT Guidelines was a proportionate measure in ensuring the availability of sufficient domestic stock of PPE products. The measure was validly enacted, in pursuance of legitimate state interest and did not disproportionately impact the fundamental rights of the Appellant. Hence, Clause 2(iii) passes muster under Articles 14, 19(1)(g) and 21.[58]

CHAPTER THREE

Atul Commodities Pvt. Ltd. and Ors. vs. Commissioner of Customs, Cochin-9 (24.02.2009 - SC) : MANU/SC/1401/2009

Relative Section:

Customs Act, 1962 - Section 111(d), Customs Act, 1962 - Section 124; Foreign Trade Development And Regulation Act, 1992 - Section 15, Foreign Trade Development And Regulation Act, 1992 - Section 16, Foreign Trade Development And Regulation Act, 1992 - Section 19, Foreign Trade Development And Regulation Act, 1992 - Section 3, Foreign Trade Development And Regulation Act, 1992 - Section 5, Foreign Trade Dev. And Regulation Act, 1992 - Section 6, Foreign Trade Development And Regulation Act, 1992 - Section 6(3)

Hon'bleJudges/Coram: S.H. Kapadia and H.L. Dattu, JJ.

Equivalent Citation: 2009(168)ECR1(SC), JT2009(4)SC23, 2009(3)SCALE242, (2009)5SCC46, [2009]3SCR589, 2009(7)UJ3189

Case Reference: nil

NumberofPagesintheOriginalJudgment: 15

Case Note:

Customs - Confiscation - Section 111(d) of the Customs Act, 1962 - In January 2005 Appellant imported photocopying machines under the category "general imports" - Whether, during said period, impugned goods were "freely importable" or whether its import required a licence/ permission/certificate - Held, in the Handbook of Procedures relating to FTP, 2002-07 it was provided that import of second-hand capital goods, not more than 10 years old, would be allowed freely (para 2.33 of the Handbook) - Policy Circular Nos. 16/03 and 19/03 pertain to period prior to January 2005 - Both the said circulars referred to FTP, 2002-07, wherein the Handbook (2002-07) it was inter alia provided that old and used capital goods which were not more than 10 years old could be imported freely, whereas Appellant imported the machines under FTP, 2004-09 - Para 2.33 of the Handbook of Procedures (2004-09) has been completely recasted - Therefore, Policy Circular Nos. 16/03 and 19/03 has no application to the facts of the present case - Import of photocopying machines stand restricted only on and after 19th October, 2005 vide Notification No. 31 as amendment by Central Government under Section 5 of the 1992 Act - Appeal allowed

Facts:

1.The facts lie within a very narrow compass.

2. In exercise of the powers conferred under Section 5 of the Foreign Trade (Development and Regulation) Act, 1992, the Central Government notified Foreign Trade Policy ("FTP" for short) for the period 2004-09 incorporating the Exim Policy for the period 2002-07 as modified. The Policy was announced on 31.8.2004. It came into force with effect from 1.9.2004. It remains in force up to 31.3.2009, unless otherwise specified.

3. The appellant imported in January, 2005 Photocopying Machines under the category "general imports".

4. On 25.2.2005, the Dy. CoC (Import) issued a show cause notice under Section 124 of the Customs Act alleging that the Used Photocopying Machines were restricted items for import under para 2.17 of the current FTP 2004-09 read with circular No. 20 : MANU/DGFT/0047/2005 dated 23.2.2005 issued by DGFT. In the show cause notice, it was thus alleged that goods have been imported without a valid import licence and consequently, they were liable to be confiscated under Section 111(d) of the Customs Act, 1962 read with para 2.17 of the FTP (2004-09).

Held, while allowing the appeal:

1. One more aspect needs to be mentioned. Para 2.33 expressly states that import of old and used computers /second-hand computers are restricted. Para 2.33 of the Handbook do not restrict photocopying machines. Import of photocopying machines are expressly restricted only by Notification No. 31 : MANU/ DGFT/ 0226/2005 dated 19.10.2005. This

itself indicates that categorization/re-categorization cannot be done by policy circulars. Such exercise has to be undertaken by specific amendment to the Policy vide Section 5 of the 1992 Act. In this case, Notification No. 31 : MANU/DGFT/0226/2005 dated 19.10.2005 indicates that the Central Government has brought in photocopying machines into the category of second-hand goods vide amendatory Notification, therefore, import of photocopying machines stand restricted only on and after 19.10.2005. In fact, if the argument of the Department is to be accepted, then there was no need to issue Notification No. 31 : MANU/DGFT/0226/2005 dated 19.10.2005.[21]

2.For the aforestated reasons,we set aside the impugned judgment of the High Court and we restore the decision of the Larger Bench of the Tribunal dated 11.5.2005 in the case of Atul Commodities Pvt. Ltd.v.CC .[22]

3. Accordingly, we allow the civil appeal filed by the assessee with no order as to costs.[23]

4. These civil appeals are filed by the Department against the judgment and order dated 15.1.2007 of the Calcutta High Court upholding the view expressed by the Larger Bench of CESTAT in the case of M/s Atul Commodities Pvt. Ltd. v. CC.[24]

5. For the reasons given by us in Civil Appeal No. 2999/07, hereinabove, we dismiss all the three civil appeals filed by the Department with no order as to costs.[25]

CHAPTER FOUR

Director General of Foreign Trade and Ors. vs. Kanak Exports and Ors. (27.10.2015 - SC) : MANU/SC/1258/2015

Relative Section:

Foreign Trade Development and Regulation Act, 1992 - Section 3, Foreign Trade Development and Regulation Act, 1992 - Section 3(2), Foreign Trade Development and Regulation Act, 1992 - Section 5, Foreign Trade Development and Regulation Act, 1992 - Section 6, Foreign Trade Development and Regulation Act, 1992 - Section 6(3), Foreign Trade Development and Regulation Act, 1992 - Section 15, Foreign Trade Development and Regulation Act, 1992 - Section 16, Foreign Trade Development and Regulation Act, 1992 - Section 19, Foreign Trade Development and Regulation Act, 1992 - Section 19(2), Foreign Trade Development and Regulation Act, 1992 - Section 90, Foreign Trade Development and Regulation Act, 1992 - Section 91, Foreign Trade Development and Regulation Act, 1992 - Section 93; Imports and Exports (Control) Act, 1947 [Repealed]; General Clauses Act, 1977 - Section 14, General Clauses Act, 1977 - Section 21; Customs Act, 1962 - Section 25, Customs Act, 1962 - Section 25(1); Bombay Rents, Hotel and Lodging House Rates Control (Gujarat Amendment) Act, 1965 - Section 29(2); Andhra Pradesh Tenancy Laws (Amendment) Act, 1979; Limitation Act, 1963 - Section 5; Delhi Co-Operative Societies Act, 1972 - Section 12, Delhi Co-Operative Societies Act, 1972 - Section 88; Code of Civil Procedure, 1908 (CPC) - Section 115; Customs Regulations; Constitution of India -

Article 14, Constitution of India - Article 19(1), Constitution of India - Article 148, Constitution of India - Article 309

Hon'bleJudges/Coram: A.K. Sikri and Rohinton Fali Nariman, JJ.

Equivalent Citation: 2015XII AD (S.C.) 325, 2015(326)ELT26(S.C.), 2015/INSC/799, 2015(12) SCALE 123, (2016)2SCC226, 2016 (4) SCJ 321, [2015]15SCR287

Case Reference:

Adani Exports Ltd. and Anr. v. Union of India and Anr. Special Civil Application No. 1676 of 2004; State of Madhya Pradesh and Ors. v. Nandlal Jaiswal and Ors. MANU/SC/0034/1986 : (1986) 4 SCC 566; R.K. Garg v. Union of India MANU/SC/0074/1981 : (1981) 4 SCC 675; Morey v. Doud 354 US 457; Metropolis Theatre Co. v. State of Chicago 57 L Ed 730; Permian Basin Area Rate 20 L Ed (2d) 312; Zippers Karamchari Union v. Union of India and Ors. MANU/SC/0572/1998 : (2000) 10 SCC 619; BALCO Employees Union (Regd.) v. Union of India and Ors. MANU/SC/ 0779/2001 : (2002) 2 SCC 333; Accountant General and Anr. v. S. Doraiswamy and Ors. MANU/SC/0407/1980 : (1981) 4 SCC 93; Kasinka Trading v. Union of India MANU/SC/0170/1995 : (1995) 1 SCC 274; Malhotra and Sons v. Union of India MANU/JK/0027/1975 : AIR 1976 J and K 41; Shrijee Sales Corporation v. Union of India MANU/SC/1099/ 1997 : (1999) 3 SCC 398; Union of India and Ors. v. Asian Food Industries MANU/SC/8538/2006 : (2006) 13 SCC 542; State of Rajasthan and Ors. v. Basant Agrotech (India) Ltd. MANU/SC/1261/2013 : (2013) 15 SCC 1; Mahabir Vegetable Oils (P) Ltd. v. State of Haryana MANU/SC/8022/2006 : (2006) 3 SCC 620; Commissioner of Income Tax v. Vatika Township Private Ltd. MANU/SC/0810/2014 : (2015) 1 SCC 1; Phillips v. Eyre (1870) LR 6 QB 1; LOffice Cherifien des Phosphates v. Yamashita-Shinnihon Steamship Co. Ltd. MANU/UKHL/0046/1993 : (1994) 1 AC 486; Keshavlal Jethalal Shah v. Mohanlal Bhagwandas and Anr. MANU/SC/0164/1968 : (1968) 3 SCR 623; Trimbak Damodhar Rajpurkar v. Assaram Hiraman Patil and Ors. MANU/SC/0344/1961 : (1962) Supp. 1 SCR 700; West v. Gwynne; Jivabhai Purshottam v. Chhagan Karson Civil Appeal No. 153 of 1958; Durlabbhai Fakirbhai v. Jhaverbhai Bhikabhai (1956) 58 BLR 85; Sakuru v. Tanaji MANU/SC/0241/1985 : (1985) 3 SCC 590; Union of India v. N.R. Parmar MANU/SC/1022/2012 : (2012) 13 SCC 340; B.S. Vadera v. Union of India MANU/SC/0160/1968 : AIR 1969 SC 118; Gopichand v. Delhi Administration MANU/SC/0056/1959 : AIR 1959 SC 609; Lachmi Narayan and Ors. v. Union of India and Ors. MANU/SC/0012/1975 : (1976) 2 SCC

953; State of Kerala and Ors. v. K.G. Madhavan Pillai and Ors. MANU/SC/
0479/1988 : (1988) 4 SCC 669; Union of India and Ors. v. Welspun India
Limited LPA No. 290 of 2007; Regional Transport Officer, Chittoor and Ors.
v. Associated Transport Madras (P) Ltd. and Ors. MANU/SC/0334/1980 :
(1980) 4 SCC 597; A.A. Calton v. Director of Education and Anr. MANU/
SC/0047/1983 : (1983) 3 SCC 33; Chairman, Railway Board and Ors. v. C.R.
Rangadhamaiah and Ors. MANU/SC/0954/1997 : (1997) 6 SCC 626

NumberofPagesintheOriginalJudgment: 74

Case Note:

Customs - Validity of Notifications - Amendment to EXIM policy -
Export Import (EXIM) Policy 2002-2007 -Framed by Central Government
- Section 5 of Foreign Trade (Development and Regulation) Act, 1992 -
Special Scheme incorporated - Provisions giving incentives to exporters
of some specified items - Amendments made vide Notification No. 28 -
Public Notice No. 40 also issued - Followed by Notification No. 38 and 40
- Government announced exclusion of export performance - Relation to
four classes of goods -Amendment unpalatable to exporters - Filed Writ
Petitions - Pending in various High Courts - Transfer petitions allowed
- Whether Notifications were issued in public interest - Whether the
Notification No. 28 is valid - Whether Notification No. 28 dated January
28, 2004 vide which Notes 1 to 5 to para 3.7.2.1 were inserted in the
EXIM Policy 2002-2007 was only clarificatory in nature or it amounted to
amendment of the provisions of para 3.7.2.1 of the EXIM Policy - Whether
Public Notice No. 40 dated January 28, 2004, issued by the DGFT, which
sought to exclude the export performance related to class of goods, is
without jurisdiction - Whether the Notifications are bad in law on the
ground that they seek to apply retrospectively - Whether, in the case of
exporters, the exports shown by them can be treated as actual exports
entitling them to avail the benefit of the Scheme - Whether para 3.7.8
of the EXIM Policy 2004-2009 and Notification Nos. 48/2005 and 8/2006
constitutionally valid

Facts:

Export Import (EXIM) Policy 2002-2007 was framed by the Central
Government Under Section 5 of the Foreign Trade (Development and
Regulation) Act, 1992 (the Act). The main purpose and objective of this
Policy was to boost the exports. In furtherance of the same, a Special
Scheme containing the provisions thereof was incorporated therein which
gave certain kind of incentives to the exporters of some specified items.

However, some amendments were made thereto vide Notification No. 28. On the same day, Public Notice No. 40(RE-2003)/2002-2007 was also issued in exercise of powers conferred under the provisions of Para 2.4 of the said Policy, which was followed by Notification No. 38 and Notification No. 40.

Vide Notification No. 28, the Central Government sought to amend certain provisions of the EXIM Policy by inserting Notes 1 to 5, which was unpalatable to the exporters of the goods mentioned therein as, according to them, under the guise of the said Notes, some benefits which had already accrued to these exporters under the EXIM Policy were taken away. Vide Public Notice No. 40, the Government announced exclusion of export performance in relation to four classes of goods mentioned in para 2 thereof from computation of the entitlement under the Scheme and, at the same time, sought to disallow the import of agricultural products falling under Chapters I to XXIV of ITC (HS) under the said scheme. Thereafter, Notification No. 38 was published Under Section 5 of the Act on the same lines on which Public Notice No. 40 was issued. The exporters of these goods, naturally, felt aggrieved thereby. There was an innocuous amendment to Notification No. 38 wherein in addition to the Director General of Foreign Trade (DGFT) as an Officer to enforce these Notifications, ex-officio Additional Secretary to the Government of India was also added. All such exporters who were affected thereby filed writ petitions in various High Courts.

The Bombay High Court has given partial relief to the exporters/writ Petitioners. The Gujarat High Court has substantially affirmed the validity of these Notifications while giving relief on one particular aspect. Insofar as judgments of Bombay High Court and Gujarat High Court are concerned, both the Union of India as well as the writ Petitioners preferred Special Leave Petitions, in which leave was granted, and these are now converted as Civil Appeals. That apart, the Single Judge of the Gujarat High Court in one of the cases dismissed the writ petition and the LPA was filed by the said Petitioner before the Division Bench of the High Court. Since the issue involved in these appeals is the same, which is raised in the LPA in the Gujarat High Court and still pending in the writ petitions filed in various High Courts, transfer petitions were filed by the Union of India seeking transfer of all those cases and to be heard along with these two appeals. Those transfer petitions were allowed. This is how all these cases are bunched together and heard simultaneously as the issue is substantially the same in all these matters.

In the transfer cases, challenge is to the constitutional validity of para 3.7.8 of the EXIM Policy 2004-2009 as well as Notification No. 48/2005 dated February 20, 2006 and Notification No. 8/2006 dated June 12, 2006 by which certain amendments in the aforesaid EXIM Policy were made. Though it involves a different Scheme, known as 'Target Plus Scheme', since the provisions and amendments are again primarily challenged on the ground that these amendments are given retrospective effect from April 01, 2005, these matters were also analogously heard with the other batch of cases.

Held, while disposing of the appeals

(1) Before adverting to the analytical discussion and deciding the validity of impugned Notifications and public notice, keeping in mind the legal principles, the Court first discussed the background in which they came to be issued. The Court observed that the main objective of the scheme was to achieve the share of 1% of global trade and accelerated growth in exports. For this purpose, the scheme intended to concentrate on the growth of certain kinds of products treating the same as "thrust sectors". In para 3.10, six such sectors are mentioned as thrust sectors, viz., Electronic hardware, Textile including garments, Auto components/ancillary, Gem and jewellery, Agriculture and service sector. It would be significant to point out that except one, all other writ Petitioners belong to Gem and jewellery sector. One writ Petitioner has export in Textile/Garments. What is highlighted is that no thrust sector was affected or prejudiced by the impugned Notification and which was primarily Gem and Jewellery exporters who got the hit. [58] and[59]

(2) As a matter of fact, immediately after the introduction of the scheme, it was found that there was unprecedented sharp rise in the export in Gem and Jewellery articles. It raised certain suspicion in the mind of the authorities as to whether these were genuine exports. The matter was investigated and on the basis of intelligence gathered by the Central Government, it was learnt that there was rampant misuse of the scheme by certain status holders. [60]

(3) The Government demonstrated that based on the exercise undertaken, Notification No. 28 as well as Public Notice No. 40 of the even date were issued. Notwithstanding strenuous efforts made by learned Counsel for the wit Petitioners to show that the exports by them were genuine and there was no misuse, the Court had no hesitation in accepting

the plea of the Union that the purport behind Notifications was bona fide which was actuated with the conditions of public interest in mind. [74] and[75]

(4) Sub-note (ii) of Note 1 now provides that export turnover of units pertaining to SEZ/EOU/EHTP/STP or products manufactured by them and exported through DTA units are not to be included and taken into account for the purpose of calculating the value of exports. Both the High Courts in the impugned judgments have held it to be clarificatory on the ground that such export turnover was excluded as these units, namely, those pertaining to SEZ/EOU/EHTP/STP schemes are getting all facilities for import without payment of duty on various types of goods including capital goods required by them for their activities and there was no intention in the original scheme also to confer double benefit under para 3.7.2.1. [83]

(5) It is difficult to accept the submission of the learned Counsel appearing for the Writ Petitioners that Note 1 which stipulated that such exports would not be counted for the purpose of entitlement was not clarificatory but an amendment to the scheme. No doubt, such EOU/EHTP/STP schemes are allowed to export goods manufactured by them through a merchant exporter/status holder recognised under the EXIM Policy. Likewise, SEZ is also authorised to export its goods through a status holder. The permission to make exports through status holder is one thing. Taking into account these exports by the status holders for the purpose of calculating the value of exports for availing the benefits of the entitlement given under the scheme is altogether different thing. The counsel for the Petitioners could not refute or deny that such SEZ/EOU//EHTP/STP are getting the benefit of the exports made by them in the form of facilities for import without payment of duty on various types of goods including capital goods required by them for their activities. [83]

(6) Therefore, exactly the same benefit which is sought to be given to the status holders for achieving incremental growth as provided in the scheme was already conferred upon. Obviously, purpose of the scheme was not to give double benefit for same exports. In fact, if that is allowed, it would be a clear case of misuse of the scheme inasmuch as for the same export turnover units operating under SEZ/EOU/EHTP/STP would get the certain incentives and the status holders also manage to extract the same benefits exploiting the scheme by exporting the goods manufactured by these STZ/EOU etc. On considering the issue in this hue, the Court agreed with the opinion of the High Court that such a sub-note (ii) was merely clarificatory

in nature. [83]

(7) Sub-note (v) to Note 1 stipulates that if the supply were made by one status holder to another status holder, these shall also be excluded while calculating the value of exports. Likewise, sub-note (vi) of Note 1 excludes the export performance made by one status holder on behalf of other status holder. High Courts have treated it as clarificatory on the ground that the Scheme was not intended to encourage the status holders/export house to pool the exports made by other exporters for the purpose of showing incremental growth in the exports and, therefore, the addition of sub-note (v) to Note 1 was in consonance with the basic objective of the scheme as originally envisaged. Having regard to the nature of this sub-note (v) and when the Court kept in mind the fact that the two status-holders if they carry out the exports and made the target as per the Scheme were entitled to the benefit of the Scheme, the Court agreed with the High Courts that even insertion of these clauses is clarificatory in nature inasmuch as it only states that the supply made by one status-holder to another status-holder will not be counted. [84]

(8) Section 5 provides that the Central Government may, from time to time, formulate and announce, the EXIM Policy. This has to be done by issuing/announcing this Policy by way of notification in the Official Gazette. The Central Government also has the power to amend the Policy so announced by adopting the same procedure i.e. by issuing notification in the Official Gazette. It is not in dispute that EXIM Policy in question was issued by notification in exercise of powers conferred Under Section 5 of the Act. This Policy, thus, is infested with statutory flavour. [90]

(9) For the purpose of carrying out the objectives of the Act which includes implementation of the Policy, Central Government is authorised to appoint DGFT as per Section 6 of the Act. Main functions of the DGFT are advising the Central Government in formulation of the Policy and he is also responsible for carrying out the said Policy. Sub-section (3) of Section 6 provides that Central Government may delegate its power exercisable under the Act. However, powers Under Sections 3, 5, 15, 16 and 19 are specifically excluded which means these powers cannot be delegated. Thus, power to announce the Policy and to amend the same remains with the Central Government. Likewise, power to make rules Under Section 19 which vests with the Central Government, cannot be delegated. [91]

(10) The question, however, is as to whether by this Public Notice, DGFT was only carrying out the EXIM Policy or this Public Notice amounted to

change in the said EXIM Policy. It is crystal clear that the Public Notice alters the provisions of EXIM Policy. It would, therefore, amount to amending the EXIM Policy, whether clarificatory or otherwise. There may be a valid justification and rational for exclusion of four items contained therein, as pleaded by the Union. However, it had to be done in accordance with law. When the DGFT had no power in this behalf, he could not have excluded such items from the purview of EXIM Policy by means of Public Notice. The power of DGFT is only to be exercised for procedural purposes and both the High Courts have rightly remarked that para 3.2.6 inserted by public notice goes beyond the procedural conditions. [94]

(11) In fact, the Government itself realised the same, namely, the DGFT had no such power. It is for this reason that what was sought to be achieved by the said Public Notice, was formalised by the Central Government by issuing Notifications dated April 21 and 23, 2004 in exercise of powers conferred on the Central Government by Section 5 of the Act and the same four items were excluded. Therefore, the Court held that the Public Notice No. 40 dated January 28, 2004 issued by DGFT, so far it excludes the four items, is ultra vires.95,96

The Notification No. 38 dated April 21, 2004 is not clarificatory in nature unlike Notification dated January 28, 2004. Therefore, the issue of retrospectivity becomes important. The Court stated at the outset that the incentive scheme in question, as promulgated by the Government, is in the nature of concession or incentive which is a privilege of the Central Government. It is for the Government to take the decision to grant such a privilege or not. It is also trite law that such exemptions, concessions or incentives can be withdrawn any time. All these are matters which are in the domain of policy decisions of the Government. When there is withdrawal of such incentive and it is also shown that the same was done in public interest, the Court would not tinker with these policy decisions. This is so laid down by catena of judgments of this Court and is now treated as established and well grounded principle of law. In such circumstances, even the Doctrine of Promissory Estoppel cannot be ignored. [100] and[101]

(12) It cannot be denied that the Government has a right to amend, modify or even rescind a particular Scheme. It is well settled that in complex economic matters every decision is necessarily empiric and it is based on experimentation or what one may call trial and error method and therefore its validity cannot be tested on any rigid prior considerations or on the application of any straight-jacket formula. [104]

The Court, in the first instance, made the legal position clear that a delegated or subordinate legislation can only be prospective and not retrospective, unless rule making authority has been vested with power under a statute to make rules with retrospective effect. In the present case, Section 5 of the Act does not give any such power specifically to the Central Government to make rules retrospective. No doubt, this Section confer powers upon the Central Government to 'amend' the policy which has been framed under the aforesaid provisions. However, that by itself would not mean that such a provision empowers the Government to do so retrospective. This legal position is rightly discussed by the Bombay High Court in the impugned judgment. [108]

(13) The effect of the aforesaid discussion would be that if the Status Holders had achieved 25% incremental growth in exports, they acquired the right to receive the benefit under the Scheme, which could not be taken away. The pertinent and crucial question is as to whether these exporters/ writ Petitioners acquired any such right? This issue would be inter-twined with other related issue, namely, whether the notification has retroactive operation or it is retrospective in nature. Both these aspects are to be dealt with simultaneously in order to provide suitable and right answer to the question posed. An astute and penetrative examination of the record, with reference to the results of the investigation, which had prompted the Central Government to issue these Notifications, provides a very tidy answer to the question posed above is that the so-called targets achieved were only on paper through fraudulent means and, therefore, it cannot be said that any vested right accrued in favour of these exporters. [109],[110] and[111]

(14) The inquiry conducted by the Government revealed that there were exports of rough diamonds even though India is not a rough diamond producing country. These exports stopped the moment DFCE benefits in respect of rough diamond were disallowed. It was also found that cut and polished diamonds were imported, stored inside a bond and re-exported with artificial value addition. Many of these exporters exported to their own counterparts in Dubai and Sharjah and when this consignments reached those destinations, they were declared as scrap to avoid import duty. [112]

(15) In such a scenario, a sagacious approach with practical sense lead the Court to conclude that these writ Petitioners/exporters had actually achieved the targets set down in the original Scheme and thereby acquired any "vested right". It was pernicious and blatant misuse of the provisions

of the Scheme and periscopic viewing thereof establishes the same. Thus, the impugned decision reflected in the notifications dated April 21 and 23, 2004, did not take away any vested right of these exporters and amendments were necessitated by over-whelming public interest/ considerations to prevent the misuse of the Scheme.114

(16) Therefore, the Court is of the opinion that even when impugned Notification issued Under Section 5 could not be retrospective in nature, such retrospectivity have not deprived the writ Petitioners/exporters of their right inasmuch as no right had accrued in favour of such persons under the Scheme. This Court, or for that matter the High Court in exercise of its writ jurisdiction, cannot come to the aid of such Petitioners/exporters who, without making actual exports, play with the provisions of the Scheme and try to take undue advantage thereof. To this extent, direction of the Bombay High Court granting these exporters benefit of the Scheme for the past period is set aside. [114]

The exporters are right in their submission that fee could not be imposed by a Public Notice and it was necessary to have recourse to Section 5 of the Act to impose such a fee. Notification dated July 24, 2003 insofar as it relates to imposition of fee is, therefore, set aside. [115]

(17) Section 5 of the Act does not empower the Government to make amendments with retrospective effect, thereby taking away the rights which have already accrued in favour of the exporters under the Scheme. No doubt, the Government has, otherwise, power to amend, modify or withdraw a particular Scheme which gives benefits to a particular category of persons under the said Scheme. At the same time, if some vested right has accrued in favour of the beneficiaries who achieved the target stipulated in the Scheme and thereby became eligible for grant of duty credit entitlement, that cannot be snatched from such persons/exporters by making the amendment retrospectively. In the present case, the Court finds that Section 5 of the Act does not give any specific power to the Central Government to make the Rules with retrospective effect. The Central Government is authorised to make Rules/Schemes under the said provision as a delegatee, which means that the EXIM Policy/Scheme framed under the said provision is by way of delegated legislation. There has to be specific power to make the amendments with retrospective effect, which are lacking in the instant case. Moreover, even if there is such a power, it cannot take away vested rights which have accrued in favour of particular persons/ exporters.128

(18) TPS, which was introduced in EXIM Policy 2004-2009 on August 31, 2004, adopted some of the features of the earlier Schemes in the EXIM Policy 2002-2007 and introduced the concept of Multi-Entitlement Rates, thus, allowing higher entitlement rates for higher growth. The Multi-Entitlement Rates depended upon the quantum of incremental growth achieved by particular exporters. Vide Notification No. 32/2005 dated April 08, 2005, the Central Government amended para 3.7.8 and instead of three rates of entitlement based on growth, it prescribed one single rate, i.e. 5% of the incremental growth. The Scheme was floated to accelerate quantum growth in exports and when those star export houses achieved the quantum growth in exports, as stated in para 3.7.3, they would naturally become entitled to a particular percentage of duty credit entitlement depending upon the quantum of growth achieved. These exporters, thus, got vested right to avail the duty credit entitlement and achieve higher rate, i.e. 10% or 15%, as the case may be. Reducing the same to 5% would clearly amount to taking away their vested right with the issuing of the Notification and making them effective retrospectively. [130],[131] and[132]

(19) Likewise, no cogent explanation is coming forward for adding four items by amending para 3.7.5 vide Notification No. 48 (RE 2005)/2004-2009 dated February 20, 2006. The only argument advanced at the time of hearing was that the Government felt that benefit of TPS should not be extended to the exporters of these items. That may be a policy decision and the Government is empowered to take such a decision. If the Government realised afterwards that export of these items should not have been given the benefit of TPS and extending the benefit to now excluded items was an ill-considered move, though the Central Government was free to withdraw it in respect of such items but it could do so only prospectively, but was not entitled to do so with effect from the back date, i.e. April 01, 2005, by taking away the vested right that had already accrued in favour of exporters of these items. As a result, the Court held that Notification No. 48/2005 dated February 20, 2006 and Notification No. 8/2006 dated June 12, 2006 cannot be applied retrospectively and they would be effective only from the dates they were issued. [134]

CHAPTER FIVE

Baraka Overseas Traders vs. Director General of Foreign Trade and Ors. (11.09.2006 - SC) : MANU/SC/8481/2006

Relative Section:

Foreign Trade Development And Regulation Act, 1992 - Section 5

Hon'bleJudges/Coram:

Ashok Bhan and Markandey Katju, JJ.

Equivalent Citation: 2006(48)AIC319, 2006(202)ELT3(S.C.), JT2006(12)SC45, 2006(9)SCALE140, (2006)8SCC103, [2006]Supp(5)SCR873

NumberofPagesintheOriginalJudgment: 5

Case Reference:

Union of India and Ors. v. Chowgule & Co. Ltd. and Ors. MANU/SC/ 0047/2003

Case Note:

Commercial - endorsement of transferability - - Section 5of Foreign Trade (Development and Regulation) Act, 1992 - Duty Exemption Scheme - Clause 7.19(a) - appellant's request for endorsement of transferability of three licences in question was refused - appellant filed writ petition which was dismissed - Hence this appeal by way of Special Leave - held, under Scheme for Duty Exemption Endorsement in the EXIM POLICY advance licenses carry certain export obligations - petitioner applied for licenses under the 'no norms category' for export of Fresh Frozen Sea Foods including Shrimps and PUD, and the said licenses were granted by the

Licensing Committee - licences were transferable under the EXIM POLICY 1997-2002, which was issued under Section 5 - duty free licenses are transferable whether they are in the 'norms category' or 'no norms category' - DGFT rejected the application for endorsement of transferability on the ground that the description of the export items was wrongly shown in the 'no norms category', whereas it should have been shown in the 'norms category' - view taken by the High Court as well as the DGFT was clearly erroneous in law and liable to be set aside - DGTF is directed to endorse the transferability of the licences in question as prayed for by the appellant

Constitution - natural justice - denial of endorsement of transferability - Held, if license is granted to someone certain rights accrue to the licence holder and deprivation of such right without a hearing is violation of natural justice - Before withdrawal of such right opportunity of hearing has to be given - In present case no such opportunity was given at all - stand of respondents that grant of licence does not confer any vested right in favour of the licencee if the licence has been obtained by misrepresentation - grant of licence certainly creates certain rights in favour of the licencee and if the Licensing Authority was of the opinion that the licence was obtained by misrepresentation, then a show cause notice should have been given to the appellant, as well as an opportunity of hearing

Ratio Decidendi:

Duty free licenses are transferable whether they are in the 'norms category' or 'no norms category

If the Licensing Authority was of the opinion that the licence was obtained by misrepresentation, then a show cause notice should have been given to the appellant, as well as an opportunity of hearing

Facts:

1. The facts of the case are that to enable Indian exporters to compete effectively in the international market a scheme was framed by the Central Government named the 'Duty Exemption Scheme'. Under this Scheme, import of certain specified input items required for the manufacture and export of resultant products was allowed with duty exemption benefits. For getting this benefit, the applicant exporter had to apply for licence with the details of the input requirements. In case, the standard input/output norms (SION) for a particular export product were already notified at the relevant point of time, the licences are normally issued by the Licensing Authority concerned without making reference to the Advance Licensing Committee. In case, the SION is not fixed, the application is to be considered by the

Committee.[4]

2. The petitioner had obtained three advance licences dated 11.12.1997, 30.7.1998 and 30.7.1998 for export of 'Fresh Frozen Sea foods' including 'Shrimps' and PUDs' from the Regional Office of the Joint Director General of Foreign Trade, Hyderabad under the Export and Import Policy of 1997-2002 (in short hereinafter referred to as 'EXIM POLICY'). These advance licences were issued for import of items such as LDPE/HDPE/ PP Moulding Powder, Kraft Paper, Raw Material for Fish Net, PP Moulding Powder/Nylon Moulding Powder/Nylon Monofilament, Anti-oxidants viz., Gentamycin Sulphate, Tetracyclene HCL, Raw Material for Tubs, Basins, Crats, etc. i.e. HDPE/PP Moulding Powder, Anti-bacterial/Anti-fungal material to increase the shelf life i.e. Tetracyclene HCL used during fishing in ice, Soya Meal, Lecithin, Wheat Gluton, Gum Arabic, Beta-Methazone/ Dexamethazone.[5]

Against all the aforesaid three advance licenses the appellant filed three separate applications all dated 16.9.98 requesting for an endorsement of transferability after fulfillment of the stipulated export obligation. The DGFT, vide order dated 19.2.1999, refused the request of the appellant for an endorsement of the transferability of the advance licenses. Against the order of the DGTF dated 19.2.1999, the appellant filed a writ petition in the High Court, which was dismissed. Hence, this appeal by way of Special Leave.

Held, while allowing the appeal:

1. It is well settled that rights which have accrued under the old law continue to exist unless there is an express or implied inconsistent provision in the new law vide 'Principles of Statutory Interpretation' by Justice G.P. Singh, 9th Edition (2004) p. 586. We find no material inconsistency between the EXIM POLICY of 1997-2002 and that of 2002-2007 so far as the matter in question is concerned.[11]

2. For the reasons given above, this appeal is allowed. The impugned judgment of the High Court dated 24.3.2000 as well as the order of the DGTF dated 19.2.1999 are set aside. The DGTF is directed to endorse the transferability of the licences in question as prayed for by the appellant. There shall be no order as to costs.[12]

CHAPTER SIX

Commissioner of Customs vs. Atul Automations Pvt. Ltd. and Ors. (24.01.2019 - SC) : MANU/SC/0067/2019

Relative Section:

Foreign Trade (Development and Regulation) Act, 1992 - Section 3, Foreign Trade (Development and Regulation) Act, 1992 - Section 3(3), Foreign Trade (Development and Regulation) Act, 1992 - Section 5, Foreign Trade (Development and Regulation) Act, 1992 - Section 11(8), Foreign Trade (Development and Regulation) Act, 1992 - Section 11(9), Foreign Trade (Development and Regulation) Act, 1992 - Section 18A; Customs Act, 1962 - Section 11; Customs Act, 1962 - Section 112, Customs Act, 1962 - Section 114AA, Customs Act, 1962 - Section 125; Hazardous and Other Wastes (Management and Transboundary Movement) Rules, 2016 - Rule 3(1)(23), Hazardous and Other Wastes (Management and Transboundary Movement) Rules, 2016 - Rule 13, Hazardous and Other Wastes (Management and Transboundary Movement) Rules, 2016 - Rule 13(2), Hazardous and Other Wastes (Management and Transboundary Movement) Rules, 2016 - Rule 15, Hazardous and Other Wastes (Management and Transboundary Movement) Rules, 2016 - Rule 15(1)(2); Foreign Trade (Regulation) Rules, 1993 - Rule 17(2)

Hon'bleJudges/Coram:

Ranjan Gogoi, C.J.I., Navin Sinha and K.M. Joseph, JJ.

Equivalent Citation: 2019(365)ELT465(S.C.), 2019(9)FLT184, 2019/INSC/90, 2019(1)SCALE686, (2019)3SCC539, 2019 (10) SCJ 390

NumberofPagesintheOriginalJudgment: 6
Case Reference: nil
Case Note:
Customs - Release of goods - Direction - Sections 3 and 5 of the Foreign Trade Act, 1992; Section 11, 125 of Customs Act, 1962; Section 11(8) and (9) read with Rule 17(2) of Foreign Trade (Regulation) Rules, 1993 - Appeal was against order of High Court holding that, MFDs were not prohibited but restricted items for import and directed release of goods subject to execution of a simple bond without sureties for 90% of enhanced assessed value - Whether impugned order of High Court directing release of goods was sustainable.

Facts:
Respondents during October-November, 2016 imported certain consignments of Multi-Function Devices (Digital Photocopiers and Printers) (MFDs). Commissioner of Customs held that, imports were in violation of Foreign Trade Policy framed under Foreign Trade (Development and Regulation) Act, 1992 and Rule 15(1)(2) of Hazardous and Other Wastes (Management and Transboundary Movement) Rules, 2016. Redemption fine was imposed under Section 125 of Customs Act, 1962 and consignment released for re-export only. Penalty was also imposed under Section 112(a) along with penalty under Section 114AA of Customs Act as also penalty was imposed on Directors. In appeal before the Tribunal, Tribunal held that, MFDs did not constitute "waste" under Rule 3(1)(23) of Waste Management Rules and had a utility life of 5 to 7 years, as certified by Chartered Engineer. Release of consignment was directed under Section 125 of Customs Act as Respondents were held to have substantially complied with requirements of Rule 13 of Waste Management Rules read with Schedule VIII Entry 4(j) except for country of origin certificate. Tribunal further noticed that, earlier also similar consignments of Respondent and others had been released at Calcutta, Chennai and Cochin ports upon payment of redemption fine. Redemption fine was reduced as also penalty under Section 112(a) of Customs Act was reduced including that on Director also. Penalty under Section 114AA was done away with. In appeal preferred by Revenue, High Court held that, MFDs correctly fell in category of "other wastes" under Rule 3(1)(23) of Waste Management Rules read with Part B and Part D of Schedule III Item B1110 dealing with used Multi-Function Printer and Copying Machines. Adverting to provisions of Foreign Trade Act and Foreign Trade Policy framed thereunder, it was

held that, MFDs were not prohibited but restricted items for import. Section 11(8) and (9) of Foreign Trade Act provided for confiscation and redemption of goods imported without authorisation upon payment of market value. Order for release of goods was upheld subject to execution of a simple bond without sureties for 90% of enhanced assessed value, with further liberty to Director General of Foreign Trade (the DGFT), along with directions.

Held, while dismissing the appeal

1. MFDs were imported in October-November 2016. They were detained by customs authorities opining that, imports had been made in violation of Foreign Trade Policy, 2015-2020 framed under Sections 3 and 5 of the Foreign Trade Act and Wastes Management Rules. [7]

2. Clause 2.01 of Foreign Trade Policy provided for prohibition and restriction of imports and exports. Export or import of restricted goods could be made under Clause 2.08 only in accordance with an authorisation/ permission to be obtained under Clause 2.11. Photocopier machines/Digital multifunction Print and Copying Machines were restricted items importable against authorisation under Clause 2.31. Indisputably, Respondents did not possess necessary authorisation for their import. Customs authorities therefore prima facie could not be said to be unjustified in detaining consignment. Merely because earlier on more than one occasion, similar consignments of Respondent or others might have been cleared by customs authorities at Calcutta, Chennai or Cochin ports on payment of redemption fine could not be a justification simpliciter to demand parity of treatment for present consignment also. Defence that, DGFT had declined to issue such authorisation did not appeal to the Court. [8]

3. Unfortunately, both Commissioner and Tribunal did not advert to provisions of Foreign Trade Act. High Court dealing with same had aptly noticed that Section 11(8) and (9) read with Rule 17(2) of Foreign Trade (Regulation) Rules, 1993 provided for confiscation of goods in event of contravention of Act, Rules or Orders but which might be released on payment of redemption charges equivalent to market value of the goods. Section 3(3) of Foreign Trade Act provided that, any order of prohibition made under the Act shall apply mutatis mutandis as deemed to have been made under Section 11 of Customs Act also. Section 18A of Foreign Trade Act reads that, it was in addition to and not in derogation of other laws. Section 125 of Customs Act vested discretion in authority to levy fine in lieu of confiscation. MFDs were not prohibited but restricted items for

import. A harmonious reading of statutory provisions of Foreign Trade Act and Section 125 of the Customs Act would therefore not detract from redemption of such restricted goods imported without authorisation upon payment of market value. There would exist a fundamental distinction between what was prohibited and what was restricted. There was no error with conclusion of Tribunal affirmed by High Court that, Respondent was entitled to redemption of consignment on payment of market price at reassessed value by customs authorities with fine under Section 112(a) of Customs Act, 1962. [9]

4. Central Government had permitted import of used MFDs with utility for at least five years keeping in mind that, they were not being manufactured in country. Chartered Engineer commissioned by customs authorities had certified that, MFDs were capable of utility for next 5 to 7 years without any major repairs. Considering that at import they had utility, the High Court rightly classified them as "other wastes" under Rule 3(1)(23) of the Waste Management Rules. [10]

5. Rule 13(2) provided procedure for import of other wastes listed in Part D Schedule III. Item B1110 of Schedule mentions used Multifunction Print and Copying Machines (MFDs). Entry 4(j) lists out five documents required for import of used MFDs. Respondents had been found to be substantially compliant in this regard and requirement for the country of origin certificate has been found to be vague by High Court. Form 6 had rightly been held to be not applicable to subject goods. [11]

6. Rule 15 of Waste Management Rules dealing with illegal traffic, provided that import of "other wastes" shall be deemed illegal if it was without permission from Central Government under Rules and was required to be re-exported. Significantly the Customs Act does not provide for re-export. Central Government under Foreign Trade Policy had not prohibited but restricted import subject to authorisation. High Court therefore rightly held that, MFDs having a utility period, Extended Producer Responsibility would arise only after utility period was over. In any event, E-waste Rules 2016 certificate had since been issued to Respondents by Central Pollution Control Board before goods had been cleared. [12]

7. There was no reason to interfere with impugned orders. In statutory scheme of Foreign Trade Act, there was no error in penultimate direction to Respondents for deposit of bond without sureties for 90% of enhanced valuation of goods leaving it to DGFT to decide whether confiscation needed to be ordered or release be granted on redemption at market value,

in which event Respondents shall be entitled to set off. [13]

8. Appeals dismissed. [14]

CHAPTER SEVEN

NKGSB Cooperative Bank Limited vs. Subir Chakravarty and Ors. (25.02.2022 - SC) : MANU/SC/0247/2022

Relative Section:

Andhra Pradesh Reorganisation Act, 2014 - Section 86; Arms Act 1959 - Section 24A, Arms Act 1959 - Section 24B, Arms Act 1959 - Section 43; Army Act, 1950 - Section 47; Banning Of Unregulated Deposit Schemes Act, 2019 - Section 31; Bihar Reorganisation Act, 2000 - Section 80; Central Goods And Services Tax Act, 2017 - Section 107, Central Goods And Services Tax Act, 2017 - Section 108, Central Goods And Services Tax Act, 2017 - Section 112, Central Goods And Services Tax Act, 2017 - Section 5; Central Reserve Police Force Act 1949 - Section 2(g); Chemical Weapons Convention Act, 2000 - Section 22, Chemical Weapons Convention Act, 2000 - Section 23, Chemical Weapons Convention Act, 2000 - Section 24, Chemical Weapons Convention Act, 2000 - Section 37; Child And Adolescent Labour (prohibition And Regulation) Act, 1986 - Section 17A; Children Act, 1960 - Section 56; Code of Civil Procedure, 1908 (CPC) - Order XXVI Rule 17; Code of Criminal Procedure, 1973 (CrPC) - Section 12; Section 154; Section 165; Section 17; Section 284; Section 34; Section 55; Conservation Of Foreign Exchange And Prevention Of Smuggling Activities Act, 1974 - Section 12; Constitution Of India - Article 154, Article 226, Article 227, Article 311, Article 311(1), Article 53; Customs Act, 1962 - Section 129D, Section 129DA, Section 28J, Section 5; Delhi Police Act, 1978 - Section 12, Section 122, Section 147,Section 20, Section 21, Section

25, Section 3, Section 58,Section 64, Section 70; Delhi Rent Act, 1995 - Section 44; Employee's Compensation Act, 1923 - Section 2(1), Employee's Compensation Act, 1923 - Section 2(f); Export (quality Control And Inspection) Act, 1963 - Section 10K, Export (quality Control And Inspection) Act, 1963 - Section 10M, Export (quality Control And Inspection) Act, 1963 - Section 13; Food Safety And Standards Act, 2006 - Section 30; Foreign Trade (development And Regulation) Act, 1992 - Section 11, Foreign Trade (development And Regulation) Act, 1992 - Section 15, Foreign Trade (development And Regulation) Act, 1992 - Section 16, Foreign Trade (development And Regulation) Act, 1992 - Section 6; Fugitive Economic Offenders Act, 2018 - Section 8; General Clauses Act 1897 - Section 3(5); Guardians And Wards Act, 1890 - Section 4A; Hotel-receipts Tax Act, 1980 - Section 23; Human Immunodeficiency Virus And Acquired Immune Deficiency Syndrome (prevention And Control) Act, 2017 - Section 45; Indian Coconut Committee Act, 1944 - Section 2(a); Indian Evidence Act, 1872 - Section 121; Indian Penal Code 1860, (IPC) - Section 165; Indian Penal Code 1860, (IPC) - Section 376; Indian Succession Act, 1925 - Section 195; Industrial Disputes Act, 1947 - Section 39; Industrial Employment (standing Orders) Act, 1946 - Section 14A; Industrial Relations Code, 2020 - Section 100; Insurance Act, 1938 - Section 110A, Insurance Act, 1938 - Section 110B, Insurance Act, 1938 - Section 34H; Legal Metrology Act, 2009 - Section 54; Mahatma Gandhi National Rural Employment Guarantee Act, 2005 - Section 26; Maintenance And Welfare Of Parents And Senior Citizens Act 2007 - Section 22; Manipur Land Revenue And Land Reforms Act, 1960 - Section 166, Manipur Land Revenue And Land Reforms Act, 1960 - Section 5, Manipur Land Revenue And Land Reforms Act, 1960 - Section 68, Manipur Land Revenue And Land Reforms Act, 1960 - Section 7, Manipur Land Revenue And Land Reforms Act, 1960 - Section 84, Manipur Land Revenue And Land Reforms Act, 1960 - Section 93, Manipur Land Revenue And Land Reforms Act, 1960 - Section 95, Manipur Land Revenue And Land Reforms Act, 1960 - Section 96; Narcotic Drugs And Psychotropic Substances Act, 1985 - Section 41; National Security Act, 1980 - Section 14; New Delhi Municipal Council Act, 1994 - Section 328, New Delhi Municipal Council Act, 1994 - Section 46; Orphanages And Other Charitable Homes (supervision And Control) Act, 1960 - Section 5; Passports Act, 1967 - Section 21; Police Act, 1861 - Section 2, Police Act, 1861 - Section 7; Prevention Of Illicit Traffic In Narcotic Drugs And Psychotropic Substances Act, 1988 - Section 13; Prevention

Of Money-laundering Act, 2002 - Section 17; Prisons Act, 1894 - Section 22, Prisons Act, 1894 - Section 48, Prisons Act, 1894 - Section 8; Punjab Reorganisation Act, 1966 - Section 79; Railways Act, 1989 - Section 93; Requisitioning And Acquisition Of Immovable Property Act, 1952 - Section 17, Requisitioning And Acquisition Of Immovable Property Act, 1952 - Section 23; Right To Fair Compensation And Transparency In Land Acquisition, Rehabilitation And Resettlement Act, 2013 - Section 43; Securitisation And Reconstruction Of Financial Assets And Enforcement Of Security Interest Act, 2002 - Section 13, Securitisation And Reconstruction Of Financial Assets And Enforcement Of Security Interest Act, 2002 - Section 13(2), Securitisation And Reconstruction Of Financial Assets And Enforcement Of Security Interest Act, 2002 - Section 13(4), Securitisation And Reconstruction Of Financial Assets And Enforcement Of Security Interest Act, 2002 - Section 14, Securitisation And Reconstruction Of Financial Assets And Enforcement Of Security Interest Act, 2002 - Section 14(1), Securitisation And Reconstruction Of Financial Assets And Enforcement Of Security Interest Act, 2002 - Section 14(1-A), Securitisation And Reconstruction Of Financial Assets And Enforcement Of Security Interest Act, 2002 - Section 14(1A), Securitisation And Reconstruction Of Financial Assets And Enforcement Of Security Interest Act, 2002 - Section 14(2), Securitisation And Reconstruction Of Financial Assets And Enforcement Of Security Interest Act, 2002 - Section 14(3), Securitisation And Reconstruction Of Financial Assets And Enforcement Of Security Interest Act, 2002 - Section 38, Securitisation And Reconstruction Of Financial Assets And Enforcement Of Security Interest Act, 2002 - Section 6(b); Security Interest (enforcement) Rules, 2002 - Rule 2(a), Security Interest (enforcement) Rules, 2002 - Rule 8, Security Interest (enforcement) Rules, 2002 - Rule 8(3), Security Interest (enforcement) Rules, 2002 - Rule 9; Suppression Of Immoral Traffic In Women And Girls Act, 1956 - Section 14; Unlawful Activities (prevention) Act, 1967 - Section 42, Unlawful Activities (prevention) Act, 1967 - Section 43A; Uttar Pradesh Consolidation Of Holdings Act, 1953 - Section 48; Uttar Pradesh Reorganisation Act, 2000 - Section 81; Wild Life (protection) Act, 1972 - Section 5

Hon'bleJudges/Coram:
A.M. Khanwilkar and C.T. Ravikumar, JJ.
Equivalent Citation: 2022(3)ABR182, 2022(233)AIC220, AIR2022SC1325, 2022(2)ALLMR854, I(2022) BC612(SC),

2022(2)BomCR410, 2022 (1) CCC 381 , 2022GLH(2)1, 2022/INSC/238, 2022(2)RCR(Civil)414, (2022)10SCC286, 2022 (2) SCJ 319, [2022]171SCL310(SC), [2022]1SCR1177

NumberofPagesintheOriginalJudgment:25

Case Reference:

Muhammed Ashraf and Ors. v. Union of India (UOI) MANU/KE/0456/2008; Federal Bank Limited v. A.V. Punnus MANU/KE/1086/2013; Sakiri Vasu v. State of U.P. and Ors. MANU/SC/8179/2007; Dattatreya Moreshwar Pangarkar v. The State of Bombay and Ors. MANU/SC/0014/1952; Sangram Singh v. Election Tribunal, Kotah and Ors. MANU/SC/0044/1955; A.S.T. Arunachalam Pillai v. Southern Roadways (Private) Ltd. MANU/SC/0249/1960; S. Krishnaswamy Mudaliar and Ors. v. P.S. Palani Pillai and Ors. MANU/TN/0237/1957; B. Veeraswamy and Ors. v. State of Andhra Pradesh represented by its Secretary, Public Works and Transport Department, Hyderabad and Ors. MANU/AP/0192/1959; R.G. Jacob v. Union of India (UOI) MANU/SC/0140/1962; Government of A.P. and Ors. v. N. Ramanaiah MANU/SC/0815/2009; Raghunath Sahai v. Sarup Singh MANU/UP/0147/1962; Ram Narain and Ors. v. Director of Consolidation and Ors. MANU/UP/0050/1965; Laxminarayan Sarangi v. State of Orissa and Ors. MANU/OR/0002/1963; Mahadev Prasad Roy v. S.N. Chatterjee and Ors. MANU/BH/0097/1954; Gurmukh Singh v. Union of India (UOI), New Delhi MANU/PH/0102/1963; Rao Shiv Bahadur Singh and Ors. v. The State of Vindhya Pradesh MANU/SC/0081/1953; Lalit Mohan Das v. Advocate-General, Orissa MANU/SC/0019/1956; O.P. Sharma and Ors. v. High Court of Punjab and Haryana MANU/SC/0571/2011; Satheedevi v. Prasanna and Ors. MANU/SC/0367/2010; Hiralal Rattanlal and Ors. v. State of U.P. and Ors. MANU/SC/0553/1972; Dipak Babaria and Ors. v. State of Gujarat and Ors. MANU/SC/0052/2014; V.S. Sunitha v. Federal Bank Ltd.; S. Chandramohan and Anr. v. The Chief Metropolitan Magistrate, Egmore, Chennai and Ors. MANU/TN/2503/2014 : 2014-5-L.W. 620; Rahul Chaudhary v. Andhra Bank and Ors.; J. Marks Exim (India) Pvt. Ltd. v. Punjab National Bank; Mahadev Govind Gharge and Ors. v. Special Land Acquisition Officer, Upper Krishna Project, Jamkhandi, Karnataka MANU/SC/0597/2011 : (2011) 6 SCC 321; Federal Deposit Ins. Corporation v. Winton, C.C.A. Tenn. MANU/FEST/0054/1942 : 131 F.2d 780; Slegel v. Slegel 135 N.J. Eq. 5 : 37 A.2d 57; Doherty v. King, Tex. Civ. App. 183 S.W.2d 1004; Donohue v. Zoning Bd. of Appeals of Town of Norwalk 155 Conn. 550 : 235 A.2d 643; Authorised Officer, Indian Bank v. D. Visalakshi and Anr.

MANU/SC/1303/2019 : (2019) 20 SCC 47

Case Note:

Banking - Possession of Secured Assets and documents - Appointment of Advocate for such purpose - Section 14(1A) of the Securitisation and Reconstruction of Financial Assets and Enforcement of Security Interest Act, 2002 - Whether District Magistrate or the Chief Metropolitan Magistrate can appoint an advocate and authorise him/her to take possession as provided for in the statute?

Facts:

The Bombay High Court vide its relevant judgment opined that the advocate, not being a subordinate officer to the CMM or DM, such appointment would be illegal. Against this decision, four separate appeals were filed by the concerned parties. On the other hand, the High Court of Madras took a contrary view that the advocate is regarded as an officer of the court and, thus, subordinate to the CMM or the DM. Against this decision, a special leave petition was filed by the borrowers.The High Courts of Kerala and Delhi have taken the same view. Hence the present appeals to adjudicate on whether Advocate can be appointment as one authorised to take possession of secured assets and connected document.

Held, while disposing the Appeals:

It is well established that an advocate is a guardian of constitutional morality and justice equally with the Judge. He has an important duty as that of a Judge. He bears responsibility towards the society and is expected to act with utmost sincerity and commitment to the cause of justice. He has a duty to the court first. As an officer of the court, he owes allegiance to a higher cause and cannot indulge in consciously misstating the facts or for that matter conceal any material fact within his knowledge.[39]

There is no reason to assume that the advocate so appointed by the CMM/DM would misuse the task entrusted to him/her and that will not be carried out strictly as per law or it would be a case of abuse of power. Rather, going by the institutional faith or trust reposed on advocates being officers of the court, there must be a presumption that if an advocate is appointed as commissioner for execution of the orders passed by the CMM/DM under Section 14(1) of the 2002 Act, that responsibility and duty will be discharged honestly and in accordance with Rules of law.[42]

A fortiori, the judgment and order of the Bombay High Court impugned in the present appealsis declared as not a good law. Whereas, the conclusion of the three High Courts, namely, High Courts of Kerala, Madras and Delhi on the question under consideration upheld.[45]

Theappeals filed by the secured creditors are allowed. Resultantly, the impugned judgment and order passed by the Bombay High Court is set aside and the subject writ petition stands dismissed.The special leave petition filed by the borrowers against the impugned judgment and order of the Madras High Court is delinked for being heard for admission, on the limited issue regarding compliance or non-compliance of Clauses (i) to (ix) of Section 14 of the 2002 Act in the fact situation of the present case.[47]

CHAPTER EIGHT

Union of India (UOI) and Ors. vs. Raj Grow Impex LLP and Ors. (17.06.2021 - SC) : MANU/SC/0369/2021

Relative Section:

Central Excise Act, 1944 - Section 35E, Section 35EE; Constitution of India - Article 142, Article 226; Customs Act, 1962 - Section 2(33), Section 11, Section 11A, Section 11B, Section 11(1), Section 11(2), Section 11(3), Section 28(2), Section 28AB, Section 49, Section 111, Section 111(d), Section 112(a),Section 113,Section 113(d), Section 124, Section 125,Section 125(1),Section 125(2),Section 129A, Section 129A(4), Section 129D, Section 129DD, Section 129D(1), Section 129D(2); Finance Act, 2018; Foreign Exchange Regulation Act, 1973; Foreign Trade (Development and Regulation) Amendment Act, 2010; Foreign Trade (development And Regulation) Act, 1992 - Section 3,Section 3(2), Section 3(3),Section 6(3),Section 9A, Section 11(9); Import (Control) Order, 1955; Imports And Exports (control) Act, 1947 - Section 3, Section 3(1)

Hon'bleJudges/Coram:

A.M. Khanwilkar, Dinesh Maheshwari and Krishna Murari, JJ.

Equivalent Citation: AIR2021SC2993, 2021(4)BomCR220, 2021(377)ELT145(S.C.), 2021/INSC/307, 2021 (5) SCJ 55, [2021]12SCR371

NumberofPagesintheOriginalJudgment: 67

Case Reference:

Garg Woollen Mills (P) Ltd. v. Addl. Collector of Customs, New Delhi MANU/SC/1087/1999; Sant Raj and Ors. v. O.P. Singla and Ors. MANU/SC/0231/1985; Reliance Airport Developers Pvt. Ltd. v. Airports Authority of India and Ors. MANU/SC/4912/2006; Mohd. Omer v. Collector of Customs, Calcutta and Ors. MANU/SC/0216/1970; Commissioner of Custom, New Delhi v. Brooks International and Ors. MANU/SC/2537/2007; Om Prakash Bhatia v. Commissioner of Customs, Delhi MANU/SC/0454/2003; P.T.R. Exports (Madras) Pvt. Ltd. and Ors. v. Union of India (UOI) and Ors. MANU/SC/0943/1996; S.B. International Ltd. and Ors. v. Asstt. Director General of Foreign Trade and Ors. MANU/SC/1079/1996; Commissioner of Customs v. Atul Automations Pvt. Ltd. and Ors. MANU/SC/0067/2019; Hargovind Das K. Joshi and Ors. v. Collector of Customs and Ors. MANU/SC/0331/1987; Horizon Ferro Alloys Pvt. Ltd. and Ors. v. Union of India and Ors. MANU/PH/1115/2016; U.P. State Road Transport Corporation and Ors. v. Mohd. Ismail and Ors. MANU/SC/0266/1991; Dorab Cawasji Warden v. Coomi Sorab Warden and Ors. MANU/SC/0161/1990; Union of India and Ors. v. Agricas LLP and Ors.; Raj Prakash Chemical v. Union of India; Raj Grow Impex LLP v. Union of India and Ors. Writ Petition (L) No. 3502 of 2020; Harihar Collections v. Union of India and Ors. Writ Petition (L) No. 3503 of 2020; Shri Amman Dhall Mill v. Commissioner of Customs; Commissioner of Customs (Import), Mumbai v. Finesse Creation Inc. (2009) 248 ELT 122; Assistant Commissioner (CT) LTU, Kakinada and Ors. v. Glaxo Smith Kline Consumer Health Care Limited; Films Rover International Ltd. and Ors. v. Cannon Film Sales Ltd. MANU/UKCH/0014/1986 : (1986) 3 All ER 772

Case Note:

Customs - Confiscation - Release of goods - Section 125 of the Customs Act, 1962 - Restriction of import of beans, peas and pulses - Notifications in connection therewith issued under the Foreign Trade (Development and Regulation) Act, 1992 (FTDR Act) and consequential Trade Notices by the Directorate General of Foreign Trade (DGFT) - Appellants aggrieved by directions issued by the High Court release of the goods imported by the private Respondents - Appellants contended goods as liable to absolute confiscation - Whether goods confiscated in the given circumstances liable for absolute confiscation or to be released?

Facts:

In the instant case, Central Government issued notifications dated 05.08.2017 and 21.08.2017, revising the policy for import of urad/moong and pigeon peas/toor dal from "free" to "restricted". Then, by the notification dated 25.04.2018, import of the said beans/pulses was to remain restricted requiring a prior licence. In challenge made against thereto, several other writ petitions were filed before different High Courts challenging the restrictions on import of these beans/peas/pulses and various interim orders were passed, staying the notifications. Writ petitions were dismissed by different High Courts. The order passed by Gujarat High Court was challenged before the Supreme Court (Special Leave Petition (C) No. 1922 of 2019) but, the same was also dismissed. Thereafter, the Central Government amended import policy conditions relating to various items of Chapter 7 of the Indian Trade Classifications (Harmonized System) 2017, Schedule I by way of SO Nos. 1478(E), 1479(E), 1480(E) and 1481(E) dated 29.03.2019. These notifications were subject matter of controversy in the instant matter. Several writ petitions were filed before various High Courts wherein interim orders were passed, permitting importers to import the said peas/pulses, notwithstanding the fact that they had not been issued the import licences. In said circumstances, Union of India approached Supreme Court with several transfer petitions. Writ petitions concerning notifications in question were withdrawn to this Court and ultimately dismissed.Respondents subsequently imported subject Goods which however came to be confiscatedpursuant to Notifications in place. Respondents were subjected to pay customs duty besides fine in order to get the goods redeemed. DGFT, however, declined to release confiscated goods. High Court in challenge made against thereto, directed Authorities to release Goods. However, authorities directed absolute confiscation of goods. High Court in challenge made against thereto stayed the order passed by Authorities. Hence, the present appeal.

Held, while allowing the Appeals:

When the matter was left for decision by the Commissioner (Appeals), there was neither any occasion nor any justification for the High Court to pass the order for release of the goods for the simple reason that any order for release of goods was to render the material part of the matter a fait accompli. This, simply, could not have been done. High Court committed a serious error in yet issuing such a writ as if the orders-in-original dated 28.08.2020 had become Rule of the Court and as if the Court was ensuring its due execution. It gets, perforce, reiterated that if the orders-in-original dated 28.08.2020 were to be executed under the mandate of the High Court, the appeals were going to be practically redundant after release of the goods and nothing material was to remain for decision by the Appellate Authority on the main subject matter of the appeal.[57]

Apart from the fundamental flaws of contradictions, the order passed by the High Court on 15.10.2020 further suffers from the shortcomings and thus, the impugned order having been passed while ignoring the relevant considerations, cannot be approved.[59]

The orders-in-original dated 28.08.2020 cannot be said to have been passed in a proper exercise of discretion. The Adjudicating Authority did not even pause to consider if the other alternative of absolute confiscation was available to it in its discretion as per the first part of Section 125(1) of the Customs Act and proceeded as if it has to give the option of payment of fine in lieu of confiscation. Such exercise of discretion by the Adjudicating Authority was more of assumptive and ritualistic nature rather than of a conscious as also cautious adherence to the applicable principles. The Appellate Authority, on the other hand, has stated various reasons as to why the option of absolute confiscation was the only proper exercise of discretion in the present matter. The reasons assigned by the Appellate Authority, to be fully in accord with the principles of exercise of discretion, as indicated hereinabove and in view of the facts and peculiar circumstances of this case.[80]

The sum and substance of the matter is that as regards the imports in question, the personal interests of the importers who made improper imports are pitted against the interests of national economy and more particularly, the interests of farmers. This factor alone is sufficient to find the direction in which discretion ought to be exercised in these matters. When personal business interests of importers clash with public interest, the former has to, obviously, give way to the latter. Further, not a lengthy discussion is required to say that, if excessive improperly imported peas/pulses are allowed to enter the country's market, the entire purpose of the notifications would be defeated. The discretion in the cases of present nature, involving far-reaching impact on national economy, cannot be exercised only with reference to the hardship suggested by the importers, who had made such improper imports only for personal gains. The imports in question suffer from the vices of breach of law as also lack of bona fide and the only proper exercise of discretion would be of absolute confiscation and ensuring that these tainted goods do not enter Indian markets. Imposition of penalty on such importers; and rather heavier penalty on those who have been able to get some part of goods released is, obviously, warranted.[82]

Hence, on the facts and in the circumstances of the present case as noticed and dilated hereinabove, the discretion could only be for absolute confiscation with levy of penalty. [84]

All the submissions seeking relief in equity are required to be, and are, rejected.[86.3]

Appeals allowed and, while setting aside the orders passed by the High Court and approving the orders-in-appeal, the goods in question are to be held liable to absolute confiscation but with a relaxation of allowing re-export, on payment of the necessary redemption fine and subject to the importer discharging other statutory obligations. [96]

CHAPTER NINE

Union of India (UOI) and Ors. vs. Agricas LLP and Ors. (26.08.2020 – SC) : MANU/SC/0614/2020

Relative Section:

Constitution of India - Article 14, Constitution of India - Article 51, Constitution of India - Article 51(c), Constitution of India - Article 73, Constitution of India - Article 77, Constitution of India - Article 166, Constitution of India - Article 253; Customs Act, 1962 - Section 11; Customs Tariff Act 1975 - Section 9A; Customs Valuation Rules, 1988; Foreign Trade (development And Regulation) Act, 1992 - Section 3, Foreign Trade (development And Regulation) Act, 1992 - Section 3(1), Foreign Trade (development And Regulation) Act, 1992 - Section 3(2), Foreign Trade (development And Regulation) Act, 1992 - Section 3(3), Foreign Trade (development And Regulation) Act, 1992 - Section 3(4), Foreign Trade (development And Regulation) Act, 1992 - Section 5, Foreign Trade (development And Regulation) Act, 1992 - Section 6(1), Foreign Trade (development And Regulation) Act, 1992 - Section 6(3), Foreign Trade (development And Regulation) Act, 1992 - Section 9, Foreign Trade (development And Regulation) Act, 1992 - Section 9A, Foreign Trade (development And Regulation) Act, 1992 - Section 9A(1), Foreign Trade (development And Regulation) Act, 1992 - Section 9A(3), Foreign Trade (development And Regulation) Act, 1992 - Section 9A(4), Foreign Trade (development And Regulation) Act, 1992 - Section 11, Foreign Trade (development And Regulation) Act, 1992 - Section 11(1), Foreign Trade (development And Regulation) Act, 1992 - Section 11(2), Foreign Trade (development And Regulation) Act, 1992 - Section 12, Foreign Trade (development And Regulation) Act, 1992 - Section 13, Foreign Trade (development And Regulation) Act, 1992 - Section 14, Foreign Trade (development And Regulation) Act, 1992 - Section 15, Foreign Trade (development And Regulation) Act, 1992 - Section 16, Foreign Trade (development And Regulation) Act, 1992 - Section 18A, Foreign Trade (development And Regulation) Act, 1992 - Section 19, Foreign Trade (development And Regulation) Act, 1992 - Section 19(3); Foreign Trade (Development and Regulation) Amendment Act, 2010; Foreign Trade (Development and Regulation) Ordinance, 1992; Foreign Trade (regulation) Rules, 1993 - Rule 4; Government of India (Transaction of Business) Rules, 1961; Imports and Exports (Control) Act, 1947; Juvenile Justice Act, 1986; Safeguard Measures (quantitative Restrictions) Rules, 2012 - Rule 2, Safeguard Measures (quantitative Restrictions) Rules, 2012 - Rule 3(1), Safeguard Measures (quantitative Restrictions) Rules, 2012 - Rule 5(1), Safeguard Measures (quantitative Restrictions) Rules, 2012 - Rule 5(2), Safeguard Measures (quantitative Restrictions) Rules, 2012 - Rule 5(3), Safeguard Measures (quantitative Restrictions) Rules, 2012 - Rule 9A, Safeguard Measures (quantitative Restrictions) Rules, 2012 - Rule 10

Hon'bleJudges/Coram:
A.M. Khanwilkar, Dinesh Maheshwari and Sanjiv Khanna, JJ.

Equivalent Citation: 2020(373)ELT752(S.C.),2020/INSC/508,2021(1)JLJ1,(2021)14SCC341,2020 (9-10) SCJ 557, [2020]14SCR372

NumberofPagesintheOriginalJudgment: 41

Case Reference:
Director General of Foreign Trade and Ors. v. Kanak Exports and Ors. MANU/SC/1258/2015; Delhi International Airport Ltd. v. International Lease Finance Corpn. and Ors. MANU/SC/0282/2015; Maganbhai Ishwarbhai Patel and Ors. v. Union of India (UOI) and Ors. MANU/SC/0044/1969; In Re: The Berubari Union and Exchange of Enclaves Reference Under Article 143(1) of The Constitution of India MANU/SC/0049/1960; Rai Sahib Ram Jawaya Kapur and Ors. v. The State of Punjab MANU/SC/0011/1955; Ram Kishore Sen and Ors. v. Union of India (UOI) and Ors. MANU/SC/0052/1965; Gramophone Co. of India Ltd. v. Birendra Bahadur Pandey and Ors. MANU/SC/0187/1984; Jolly George Varghese and Ors. v. The Bank of Cochin MANU/SC/0014/1980; Associated Cement

Companies Ltd. and Ors. v. Commissioner of Customs MANU/SC/0051/2001; State of Punjab and Ors. v. Devans Modern Brewaries Ltd. and Ors. MANU/SC/0961/2003; S and S. Enterprise v. Designated Authority and Ors. MANU/SC/0126/2005; Commissioner of Customs, Bangalore v. G.M. Exports and Ors. MANU/SC/1062/2015; Entertainment Network (India) Ltd. and Ors. v. Super Cassette Industries Ltd. and Ors. MANU/SC/2179/2008; Kesavananda Bharati Sripadagalvaru v. State of Kerala MANU/SC/0445/1973; Pratap Singh v. State of Jharkhand and Ors. MANU/SC/0075/2005; Raj Parkash Chemicals Ltd. and Ors. v. Union of India (UOI) and Ors. MANU/SC/0031/1986; Karan Dileep Nevatia v. The Union of India (UOI) through the Commerce Secretary, Ministry of Commerce and Industry, MANU/MH/0001/2010; Maclaine Watson & Co. Ltd. v. Department of Trade and Industry and Anr. MANU/UKHL/0040/1989 : (1989) 3 All ER 523; People's Union for Civil Liberties v. Union of India; Madhu Kishwar v. State of Bihar; Kubic Darusz v. Union of India; Chameli Singh v. State of U.P.; C. Masilamani Mudaliar v. Idol of Sri Swaminathaswami Swaminathaswami Thirukoil; Apparel Export Promotion Council v. A.K. Chopra; Kapila Hingorani v. State of Bihar; State of Punjab v. Devans Modern Breweries Ltd.; Liverpool & London S.P. & I Assn. Ltd. v. M.V. Sea Success I; Lonrho Exports v. ECGD MANU/UKCH/0011/1996 : (1998) 3 W.L.R. 394; The Eschersheim and Anr. v. The Jade Erkowit and Anr. (1976) 1 All ER 920 (HL)

Case Note:

Customs - Validity of Notifications - Excessive delegation - S.O. Numbers. 1478E, 1479E, 1480E and 1481E dated 29th March 2019 and Trade Notices - Notifications were issued under Section 3 of the Foreign Trade (Development and Regulation) Act, 1992 - Imposition of restrictions on import of Peas and pulses -Writ Petitions challenging Notifications and Trade Notices before different High Courts dismissed - Plea of Quantitative Restrictions raised in present proceedings, while assailing orders of High Courts - Whether the impositions placed sustainable?

Facts:

Writ Petitions were filed before the Madras High Court challenging relevant Notifications and Trade Notices and several traders thereafter filed Writ Petitions before different High Courts challenging imposition of restrictions on import of Peas and pulses and interim orders were passed staying the notifications which had the effect of permitting imports without any restriction as to quota or licence. The primary grounds raised in the

Writ Petitions before the High Courts were that, (a) the impugned notifications issued by the DGFT had the effect of modifying or amending the EXIM policy but the DGFT was not authorised to authenticate/issue an order amending or modifying the EXIM policy as this power vests with the Central Government; (b) the impugned notifications were not laid before the Houses of the Parliament; (c) Notifications and trade notices suffer from the vires and defects; (d) Notifications and the trade notices offend the right to equality and violate Article 14 of the Constitution. Writ Petitions filed before different High Courts were dismissed. Despite such dismissals, more writ petitions came to be filed before several High Courts wherein in interim orders were passed permitting the importers to import Peas/pulses notwithstanding the fact that they had not been issued authorisation/import licences or the total imports would exceed the maximum or total quantity fixed in the impugned notifications. New legal issue was raised in the present proceedings not specifically raised in the Writ Petitions that the impugned notifications were in the nature of 'quantitative restrictions' under Section 9A of the FTDR Act, which could be only imposed by the Central Government after conducting necessary enquiry.

Held, while rejecting the Appeal:

The impugned notifications valid as they were issued in accordance with the power conferred in the Central Government in terms of Sub-section (2) to Section 3 of the FTDR Act. The powers of the Central Government by an order imposing restriction on imports Under Sub-section (2) to Section 3 not entirely curtailed by Section 9A of the FTDR Act. [62]

In the present case, the Court was not called upon to decide and examine the obligations of the Contracting Parties in terms of GATT-1994. [64]

Impugned notifications and trade notices were upheld and rejected the challenge made by the importers. The imports, if any, made relying on interim order(s) contrary to the notifications and the trades notices issued under the FTDR Act and would be so dealt with under the provisions of the Customs Act 1962. The Writ Petitions subject to directions dismissed. Writ Petitions filed by the intervenors before the respective High Courts were dismissed. [67]

Commnr. of Customs vs. G.P. Jaiswal and Ors. (27.03.2015 - SC) : MANU/SC/0463/2015
Relative Section:

Customs Act, 1962 - Section 2(41), Customs Act, 1962 - Section 14, Customs Act, 1962 - Section 113, Customs Act, 1962 - Section 114I, Customs Act, 1962 - Section 124; Foreign Exchange Regulation Act, 1973 [Repealed] - Section 18; Foreign Trade Development and Regulation Act, 1992 - Section 11(1); Foreign Trade (Development and Regulation) Rules, 1993 - Rule 11

Hon'bleJudges/Coram:
A.K. Sikri and Rohinton Fali Nariman, JJ.
Equivalent Citation: 2015(318)ELT610(S.C.), (2015)14SCC530
NumberofPagesintheOriginalJudgment:5
Case Reference:
Om Prakash Bhatia v. Commissioner of Customs, Delhi MANU/SC/0454/2003 : (2003) 6 SCC 161; Yash Exports Inc. v. Commissioner of Customs, Lucknow MANU/CE/0826/2004 : 2005 (179) E.L.T. 238
Case Note:

Customs - Confiscated goods - Release thereof - Exaggerated value of goods - Sections 113 and 114 of Customs Act, 1962 - Appellate Tribunal set aside Commissioner's order as it was case of over invoicing, action under under Section 113(d) of Act for confiscation of goods could not have been taken for default/breach on part of exporter - Hence, present appeal - Whether question of imposition of penalty under Section 114(I) of Act also would not arise since goods were not liable for confiscation - Held, as per present Court in case of Om Prakash Bhatia, provisions of Clause (d) of Section 113 of Act would get attracted and goods might be liable for confiscation when value of goods in invoices was exaggerated - Goods were liable for confiscation under Sub-section (d) of Section 113 of Act, and therefore penalty could be imposed under Section 114(I) of Act - Commissioner imposed order of payment of penalty upon 1st Respondent only on ground that goods were cleared for export by his son - That could hardly be ground to fasten liability or attribute abetment on part of 1st Respondent - Only allegation against 2nd Respondent was that he had supervised stuffing of goods and received payment - Only on such allegation, it could not be attributed that he became party to over invoicing of goods - Penalty in respect of these Respondents had to be set aside - Allegation which had been established against 3rd Respondent was that he had direct role in obtaining report and it was on that basis exporter fraudulently claimed high DEPB to their credit - Without such report it was not possible for exporter to fraudulently import high DEPB-Therefore, penalty against exporter was accordingly maintained -Appeal disposed of. [paras 6,8,9 & 10]

Facts:

Appellate Tribunal set aside Commissioner's order as it was case of over invoicing, action under under Section 113(d) of Act for confiscation of goods could not have been taken for default/breach on part of exporter and further, imposition of penalty under Section 114(I) of Act also would not arise since goods were not liable for confiscation. Hence, present appeal.

Held:

Release of confiscated goods:

(i) As per present Court in case of Om Prakash Bhatia, provisions of Clause (d) of Section 113 of Act would get attracted and goods might be liable for confiscation when value of goods in invoices was exaggerated. [para 6]

(ii) Goods were liable for confiscation under Sub-section (d) of Section 113 of Act, and therefore penalty could be imposed under Section 114(I) of Act. [para 8]

(iii) Commissioner imposed order of payment of penalty upon 1st Respondent only on ground that goods were cleared for export by his son. That could hardly be ground to fasten liability or attribute abetment on part of 1st Respondent. Only allegation against 2nd Respondent was that he had supervised stuffing of goods and received payment. Only on such allegation, it could not be attributed that he became party to over invoicing of goods. Penalty in respect of these Respondents had to be set aside. [para 9]

(iv) Allegation which had been established against 3rd Respondent was that he had direct role in obtaining report and it was on that basis exporter fraudulently claimed high DEPB to their credit. Without such report it was not possible for exporter to fraudulently import high DEPB. Therefore, penalty against exporter was accordingly maintained. [para 10]

CHAPTER TEN

Commnr. of Customs vs. G.P. Jaiswal and Ors. (27.03.2015 - SC) : MANU/SC/0463/2015

Relative Section:

Customs Act, 1962 - Section 2(41), Customs Act, 1962 - Section 14, Customs Act, 1962 - Section 113, Customs Act, 1962 - Section 114I, Customs Act, 1962 - Section 124; Foreign Exchange Regulation Act, 1973 [Repealed] - Section 18; Foreign Trade Development and Regulation Act, 1992 - Section 11(1); Foreign Trade (Development and Regulation) Rules, 1993 - Rule 11

Hon'bleJudges/Coram:

A.K. Sikri and Rohinton Fali Nariman, JJ.

Equivalent Citation: 2015(318)ELT610(S.C.), (2015)14SCC530

NumberofPagesintheOriginalJudgment:5

Case Reference:

Om Prakash Bhatia v. Commissioner of Customs, Delhi MANU/SC/0454/2003 : (2003) 6 SCC 161; Yash Exports Inc. v. Commissioner of Customs, Lucknow MANU/CE/0826/2004 : 2005 (179) E.L.T. 238

Case Note:

Customs - Confiscated goods - Release thereof - Exaggerated value of goods - Sections 113 and 114 of Customs Act, 1962 - Appellate Tribunal set aside Commissioner's order as it was case of over invoicing, action under under Section 113(d) of Act for confiscation of goods could not have been taken for default/breach on part of exporter - Hence, present appeal - Whether question of imposition of penalty under Section 114(I) of Act also would not arise since goods were not liable for confiscation

- Held, as per present Court in case of Om Prakash Bhatia, provisions of Clause (d) of Section 113 of Act would get attracted and goods might be liable for confiscation when value of goods in invoices was exaggerated - Goods were liable for confiscation under Sub-section (d) of Section 113 of Act, and therefore penalty could be imposed under Section 114(I) of Act - Commissioner imposed order of payment of penalty upon 1st Respondent only on ground that goods were cleared for export by his son - That could hardly be ground to fasten liability or attribute abetment on part of 1st Respondent - Only allegation against 2nd Respondent was that he had supervised stuffing of goods and received payment - Only on such allegation, it could not be attributed that he became party to over invoicing of goods - Penalty in respect of these Respondents had to be set aside - Allegation which had been established against 3rd Respondent was that he had direct role in obtaining report and it was on that basis exporter fraudulently claimed high DEPB to their credit - Without such report it was not possible for exporter to fraudulently import high DEPB-Therefore, penalty against exporter was accordingly maintained -Appeal disposed of. [paras 6,8,9 & 10]

Facts:

Appellate Tribunal set aside Commissioner's order as it was case of over invoicing, action under under Section 113(d) of Act for confiscation of goods could not have been taken for default/breach on part of exporter and further, imposition of penalty under Section 114(I) of Act also would not arise since goods were not liable for confiscation. Hence, present appeal.

Held:

Release of confiscated goods:

(i) As per present Court in case of Om Prakash Bhatia, provisions of Clause (d) of Section 113 of Act would get attracted and goods might be liable for confiscation when value of goods in invoices was exaggerated. [para 6]

(ii) Goods were liable for confiscation under Sub-section (d) of Section 113 of Act, and therefore penalty could be imposed under Section 114(I) of Act. [para 8]

(iii) Commissioner imposed order of payment of penalty upon 1st Respondent only on ground that goods were cleared for export by his son. That could hardly be ground to fasten liability or attribute abetment on part of 1st Respondent. Only allegation against 2nd Respondent was that he had supervised stuffing of goods and received payment. Only on such allegation, it could not be attributed that he became party to over invoicing of goods. Penalty in respect of these Respondents had to be set aside. [para 9]

(iv) Allegation which had been established against 3rd Respondent was that he had direct role in obtaining report and it was on that basis exporter fraudulently claimed high DEPB to their credit. Without such report it was not possible for exporter to fraudulently import high DEPB. Therefore, penalty against exporter was accordingly maintained. [para 10]

CHAPTER ELEVEN

Commissioner of Custom, New Delhi vs. Brooks International and Ors. (24.05.2007 - SC) : MANU/ SC/2537/2007

Relative Section:

Customs Act, 1962 - Section 11, Customs Act, 1962 - Section 111, Customs Act, 1962 - Section 111(d), Customs Act, 1962 - Section 113, Customs Act, 1962 - Section 113(1)(d), Customs Act, 1962 - Section 113(d), Customs Act, 1962 - Section 14, Customs Act, 1962 - Section 2, Customs Act, 1962 - Section 2(33), Customs Act, 1962 - Section 2(41), Customs Act, 1962 - Section 46, Customs Act, 1962 - Section 50, Customs Act, 1962 - Section 76, Customs Act, 1962 - Section 76(1)(b); Foreign Exchange Regulation Act, 1973 [repealed] - Section 18; Foreign Trade Development And Regulation Act, 1992 - Section 11(1); Imports And Exports (control) Act, 1947 [repealed] - Section 3

Hon'bleJudges/Coram:

Dr. Arijit Pasayat and L.S. Panta, JJ.

Equivalent Citation: 2007(119)ECC1, 2007(145)ECR1(SC), 2007(213)ELT161(S.C.), JT2007(8)SC514, 2007(3)RCR(Civil)344, 2007(8)SCALE373, (2007)10SCC396, [2007]7SCR791

NumberofPagesintheOriginalJudgment: 7

Case Reference:

Om Prakash Bhati v. Commissioner of Customs, Delhi MANU/SC/0454/
2003 : (2003) 6 SCC 161 : AIR 2003 SC 3581 : 2003 (88) ECC 457 (SC)
: 2003 (155) ELT 423 (SC) : JT 2003 (5) SC 279 : 2003 (5) SCALE 197;
Sheikh Mohd. Omer v. Collector of Customs, Calcutta and Ors. MANU/SC/
0216/1970 : (1970) 2 SCC 728 : AIR 1971 SC 293 : 1983 (13) ELT 1439
(SC) : [1971] 2 SCR 35

Case Note:

Customs - Confiscation - Redemption fine - Section 113(d) of the
Customs Act, 1962 - Market value of goods under export much less than
the amount of drawback claimed - Whether goods can be confiscated for
violation of the provisions of the Customs Act, 1962 - Commissioner
directed confiscation on account of mis-description of goods and allowed to
redeem the same on payment of fine, disallowed the export of readymade
garments and claim of drawback - On appeal, CEGAT allowed the appeals
- Appellant submitted that Section 113(1) (d) and (c) will be applicable as
Section deals with excisable goods, prohibited goods and goods entered for
exportation - Hence present petition - The market value of goods under
export much less than the amount of draw back claimed whether such
goods can be confiscated for violation of provisions of the Act - Held, where
the export value was not correctly stated, but there was intentional over-
invoicing for some other purpose, that is to say, not mentioning true sale
consideration of the goods, it would amount to violation of the conditions
for import/export of the goods - The purpose may be money laundering or
some other purpose, but it would certainly amount to illegal/unauthorized
money transaction - Over-invoicing of the export goods would result in
illegal/irregular transactions in foreign currency - It would be appropriate
for the CEGAT to rehear the appeals - Matter remitted for fresh
consideration keeping in view the principles set out in the Om Prakash case
- Impugned order set aside - Appeals partly allowed

Facts:

The Respondent had sent a consignment to the export shed for
exporting the same under claim for duty drawback. On examination by
DRI, it was noted that the goods did not appear as per description, quantity
and value disclosed in the bills. The Commissioner of Customs directed
confiscation of all the goods under Section 113(d) and (i) of the Act and
allowed to redeem of the same on payment of fine, disallowed the export of
readymade garments and claim of drawback. On appeal, the CEGAT allowed
the appeals holding that there was no power of confiscation and there was

no material placed to record to suggest that the goods did not correspond to any material entry made in the bills and the correctness of the FOB and description of the goods specified in the bills had not been disputed. Hence, the present appeal.

Held:

[1] Hence, in cases where the export value is not correctly stated, but there is intentional over-invoicing for some other purpose, that is to say, not mentioning true sale consideration of the goods, then it would amount to violation of the conditions for import / export of the goods. The purpose may be money laundering or some other purpose, but it would certainly amount to illegal/unauthorized money transaction. In any case, over-invoicing of the export goods would result in illegal/irregular transactions in foreign currency.'

[2] It would be appropriate for the CEGAT, which had not considered the effect of the Larger Bench judgment, which had approval of this Court in Om Parkash case (supra) to rehear the appeals. We, therefore, set aside the Order of the CEGAT and remit the matter to it for fresh consideration keeping in view the principles set out in the Om Parkash case (supra).

Ratio Decidendi:

"In cases where the export value is not correctly stated, but there is intentional over-invoicing for some other purpose, then it would amount to violation of the conditions for import/export of the goods."

CHAPTER TWELVE

Union of India (UOI) and Ors. vs. Asian Food Industries (07.11.2006 - SC) : MANU/ SC/8538/2006

Relative Section:

Constitution Of India - Article 14; Customs Act, 1962 - Section 11, Customs Act, 1962 - Section 16, Customs Act, 1962 - Section 16(1), Customs Act, 1962 - Section 39, Customs Act, 1962 - Section 50, Customs Act, 1962 - Section 51; Foreign Trade Development And Regulation Act, 1992 - Section 11, Foreign Trade Development And Regulation Act, 1992 - Section 3, Foreign Trade Development And Regulation Act, 1992 - Section 3(2), Foreign Trade Development And Regulation Act, 1992 - Section 5

Hon'bleJudges/Coram:

S.B. Sinha and Markandey Katju, JJ.

Equivalent Citation: AIR2007SC750, 2006(204)ELT8(S.C.), JT2007(10)SC65, 2006(12)SCALE105, (2006)13SCC542, [2006]Supp(9)SCR485

NumberofPagesintheOriginalJudgment: 10

Case Reference:

Principal Appraiser (Exports), Collectorate of Customs and Central Excise and Ors. v. Esajee Tayabally Kapasi, Calicut MANU/SC/0823/1995; Gangadhar Narsingdas Agarwal v. P.S. Thrivikraman and Anr. MANU/ SC / 0282/1972; Union of India and Ors. v. C. Damani & Co. and Ors. MANU/ SC/0266/1980; State Trading Corporation of India Ltd. v. Union of India and Ors. MANU/SC/1546/1994; U.P. Cooperative Cane Unions Federations

v. West U.P. Sugar Mills Association and Ors. MANU/SC/0455/2004; State of U.P. and Ors. v. Hindustan Aluminium Corporation and Ors. MANU/SC/ 0356/1979; Municipal Corporation of the City of Toronto v. Virgo; Talcher Municipality v. Talcher Regulated Market Committee and Anr. MANU/ SC/ 0559/2004; K. Ramanathan v. State of Tamil Nadu and Anr. MANU/SC/ 0034/1985

Case Note:

Customs - Foreign trade - Clause 1.5 of the Foreign Trade Policy issued on 7th April, 2006 - Meaning of 'restriction' and 'regulation' thereunder - Whether includes prohibition - Section 5 of Foreign Trade (Development and Regulation) Act, 1992 - Prohibitory order thereunder - Whether can be retrospective - Statutory law - Interpretation of prohibitory order - Rule of strict construction - Applicability of - On 27.06.2006 in exercise of its power under Section 5 of the Foreign Trade (Development and Regulation) Act, 1992 the Central Government prohibited export of various goods mentioned therein for a period of six months from the said date - Another notification was issued by on 4.07.2006 permitting export of pulses against irrevocable letter of credit opened prior to 22.06.2006, on which date the decision of banning export was taken - 87 containers of Respondent were cleared and Let Export Orders dated 23.06.2006, 24.06.2006 and 26.06.2006 were issued by the custom - Permission to shift the 87 containers of vessels in view of the notification dated 4.07.2006 was sought but refused - Writ petition then was filed and allowed by Gujarat High Court on the ground that customs authorities cleared and permitted the loading of the goods and moreover the bill of lading had also been filed - Agri Trade India Services P. Ltd. had also challenged the validity of notification dated 4.07.2006 and the same was allowed by the Delhi High Court declaring the notification as ultra vires - Hence present appeal - Held, "regulate" and "prohibit" inhere in them elements of restriction but it varies in degree - The element of restriction is inherent both in regulative measures as well as in prohibitive or preventive measures - Prohibition promulgated by a statutory order in terms of Section 5 read with the relevant provisions of the policy decision in the light of Sub-section (2) of Section 3 of the 1992 Act can only have a prospective effect - In construing such a prohibitory order, whereas the rule of strict construction must be followed, the interpretation which subserves the intention of the Central Government as laid down in the policy as well as in the procedure should be given effect to - Appeal against judgment of Gujarat High Court dismissed and against Delhi High Court allowed

Facts:

1. Respondent herein is exporter of various kinds of pulses and grains. It received orders for supply of 20331 MT of pulses from the Overseas Importers of Middle East wherefore several contracts were entered into. The said contracts were executed between 22.4.2006 and 2.05.2006. It received US $294942 being approximately 20% of the contract amount by way of advance towards the said supply from the importers on 9.5.2006. Shipment of 20 containers out of the 107 containers consisting of 415 MT took place during the period between 22.06.2006 and 24.06.2006. The remaining 87 containers were cleared and Let Export Orders dated 23.06.2006, 24.06.2006 and 26.06.2006 were issued by the custom authorities at Kandla Port. Bills of lading were also issued therefore.[3]

2. In the meanwhile, a purported decision was taken by the Central Government to ban export of pulses on 22.06.2006. The said decision is said to have been widely reported in the electronic media and print media, but the notification banning the export of pulses was Issued by the Central Government only on 27.06.2006 in purported exercise of its power under Section 5 of the Foreign Trade (Development and Regulation) Act, 1992 (for short "the 1992 Act") wherein the Central Government prohibited export of various goods mentioned therein for a period of six months from the said date, the relevant portion whereof reads as under:[4]

Superintendent (Customs) on or about 28.6.2006 directed the Kandla Port Trust that no further consignment be allowed to be shipped which has passed out of the charge of the customs. However, the Assistant Traffic Manager in a communication made to M/s. Intermark Shipping Agency Pvt. Ltd. dated 29.06.2006 informed that even if goods have been cleared by issuance of Let Export Orders, the same should not be loaded on the shipping vessels in view of the said prohibition.

3. Another notification was issued by the Central Government on 4.07.2006 purported to be under Section 5 of the 1992 Act permitting export of pulses against irrevocable letter of credit opened prior to 22.06.2006, the relevant portion whereof reads as under:[5]

S.O.(E) In exercise of the powers conferred by Section 5 of the Foreign Trade (Development & Regulation) Act, 1992 (No. 22 of 1992) read with Para 1.3 and Para 2.1 of the Foreign Trade Policy, 2004-2009, the Central Government hereby makes the amendment in para 3 of Notification No 15 dated 27th June 2006, to include the following sentence, at the end of the said para:

Further the transitional arrangements notified under para 1.5 of the Foreign Trade Policy, 2006 shall not be applicable for export of pulses against irrevocable Letters of Credit opened on or after 22.6.2006 as the decision of the Government prohibiting the export of pulses was announced and got widely publicised on 22.6.2006 in the electronic and print media.

The respondents, however, addressed various correspondences with the authorities to grant permission to shift the 87 containers of vessels in view of the notification dated 4.07.2006 but the same was refused. A writ petition questioning the said action on the part of the authorities filed by them in the Gujarat High Court has been allowed by reason of the impugned judgment.

FACT RE: M/S. AGRI TRADE INDIA SERVICES P. LTD.

4. M/s. Agri Trade India Services P. Ltd., Respondent No. 1 herein was awarded a contract by Trade Corporation of Pakistan for supply of 3000 MT of chick peas. An irrevocable letter of credit was opened in favour of the respondent on 24.06.2006. On 27.06.2006, the respondent filed shipping invoices and bill with customs authorities for export of chick peas. In view of notification dated 27.06.2006, the Kandla Port Trust issued instructions that loading of chick peas would not be permitted. Thereafter, a notification dated 4.7.2006 was also issued purported to be under Section 5 of the 1992 Act permitting export of pulses against irrevocable letter of credit opened prior to 22.06.2006.[6]

Inter alia questioning the validity of notification dated 4.07.2006, the respondents filed a writ petition before the Delhi High Court which was marked as W.P. (C) No. 11691-11692 of 2006. By reason of the impugned judgment dated 18.08.2006, the said writ petition has been allowed.

Held, while allowing the appeal:

1. The Delhi High Court, however, in our view correctly opined that the notification dated 4.07.2006 could not have been taken into consideration on the basis of the purported publicity made in the proposed change in the export policy in electronic or print media. Prohibition promulgated by a statutory order in terms of Section 5 read with the relevant provisions of the policy decision in the light of Sub-section (2) of Section 3 of the 1992 Act can only have a prospective effect. By reason of a policy, a vested or accrued right cannot be taken away. Such a right, therefore, cannot a fortiori be taken away by an amendment thereof.[19]

2. In construing such a prohibitory order, whereas the rule of strict construction must be followed, the interpretation which subserves the intention of the Central Government as laid down in the policy as well

as in the procedure should be given effect to. A statute as is well known may have to be construed in the light of the subordinate legislations framed thereunder. When subordinate legislation has been framed by the same authority which exercises the power under the policy, the intention of such policy maker must be found out from the words used therein albeit having regard to the rights of the exporters which are sought to be protected thereby.[20]

3. We, therefore, are of the opinion that whereas the judgment of the Gujarat High Court must be upheld, that of the Delhi High Court, albeit for different reasons, cannot be sustained.[21]

For the reasons aforementioned, whereas Civil Appeal arising out of SLP (C) No. 17008 of 2006 is dismissed with costs and counsel's fee assessed at Rs. 1,00,000/-, Civil Appeal arising out of SLP (C) No. 17558 of 2006 is allowed and the parties shall pay and bear their own costs.

Om Prakash Bhatia vs. Commissioner of Customs, Delhi (07.07.2003 - SC) : MANU/SC/0454/2003

Relative Section:

Customs Act, 1962 - Section 11, Customs Act, 1962 - Section 111, Customs Act, 1962 - Section 111(d), Customs Act, 1962 - Section 113(d), Customs Act, 1962 - Section 14, Customs Act, 1962 - Section 2, Customs Act, 1962 - Section 2(33), Customs Act, 1962 - Section 2(41), Customs Act, 1962 - Section 46, Customs Act, 1962 - Section 50, Customs Act, 1962 - Section 76; Foreign Exchange Regulation Act, 1973 [repealed] - Section 18; Foreign Trade Development And Regulation Act, 1992 - Section 11(1)

Hon'bleJudges/Coram:

M.B. Shah and Arun Kumar, JJ.

Equivalent Citation: 2003(9)AIC494, AIR2003SC3581, 2003(88)ECC457, 2003 (109) ECR336 (SC), 2003(155)ELT423(S.C.), JT2003(5)SC279, 2003(5)SCALE197, (2003)6SCC161, [2003] Supp1 SCR412

Number of Pages in the Original Judgment: 8

Case Reference:

Sheikh Mohd. Omer v. Collector of Customs, Calcutta and Ors., MANU/SC/0216/1970; Toolsidass Jewraj v. Additional Collector of Customs and Ors., MANU/SC/0253/1991; Sheikh Mohd. Omer v. CC & Ors. [1970 (2) SCC 728];Toolsidass Jewraj v. ACC & Ors. [1991 (34) ECR 1 (SC) : ECR C Cus. 1847 SC]

Case Note:

Held: Valuation of goods exported - Over invoicing to be treated as exporting prohibited goods--CTA, 1975 under Section 14 along with 2(41)--Mandatory for exporter to disclose true export value of goods--Drawback not allowed if market price of goods is less--Exporter over invoiced. Fraudently to claim drawback hence redemption fine and penalty imposed.

Facts:

1. It is stated that the appellant is engaged in the export of garments. Appellant received an order from an overseas buyer i.e. from Dubai, for supply of ladies' skirts, the contracted price for which was said to be approximately $10.25 per piece. Appellant filed 4 shipping bills in 1998 for export of 28000 pieces of ladies skirts @ $10.25 per piece (Rs. 434 per piece) amounting to Rs. 1,21,54,447/-. On checking, the actual quantity of the skirts was found to be 21184 pieces. On enquiry, the market price of the skirts was ascertained to be Rs.45/- per piece, according to which total value of the goods comes to Rs. 9,53,280/-. The exporters had claimed a drawback of Rs. 21,87,800/- on the consignment @ Rs. 78/- per piece. For shortage of goods, vide letter dated 4.2.1999, the exporters pleaded that it was an unintentional mistake which had happened on the part of the fabricators and suppliers. During the course of hearing, on 6.2.1999, for the drawback, it was admitted by the exporters that the market price of Rs. 45/- per piece was acceptable to them and that their claim for drawback be not granted. The Commissioner of Customs noted that this was the second such case belonging to the same exporters and that there was an organized racket to claim fraudulent drawback by deliberately over-invoicing the readymade garments. The Commissioner of Customs imposed a redemption fine of Rs. 10,00,000/- and levied a penalty of Rs. 20,00,000/-. It was held that no drawback was admissible even if the party exported the goods in terms of Section 76 of the Act as the market value of the goods was less than the amount of drawback claimed.[3]

2. Being aggrieved by the said order, the appellant filed appeal before the Customs, Excise and Gold (Control) Appellate Tribunal, New Delhi (hereinafter referred to as 'the Tribunal'). The Tribunal also dismissed the appeal and held that the over-invoicing of the goods for exportation was an offence under the Act. Hence, this appeal.[4]

Held, while allowing the appeal:

1. It is stated that the appellant is engaged in the export of garments. Appellant received an order from an overseas buyer i.e. from Dubai, for

supply of ladies' skirts, the contracted price for which was said to be approximately $10.25 per piece. Appellant filed 4 shipping bills in 1998 for export of 28000 pieces of ladies skirts @ $10.25 per piece (Rs. 434 per piece) amounting to Rs. 1,21,54,447/-. On checking, the actual quantity of the skirts was found to be 21184 pieces. On enquiry, the market price of the skirts was ascertained to be Rs.45/- per piece, according to which total value of the goods comes to Rs. 9,53,280/-. The exporters had claimed a draw back of Rs. 21,87,800/- on the consignment @ Rs. 78/- per piece. For shortage of goods, vide letter dated 4.2.1999, the exporters pleaded that it was an unintentional mistake which had happened on the part of the fabricators and suppliers. During the course of hearing, on 6.2.1999, for the drawback, it was admitted by the exporters that the market price of Rs. 45/- per piece was acceptable to them and that their claim for drawback be not granted. The Commissioner of Customs noted that this was the second such case belonging to the same exporters and that there was an organized racket to claim fraudulent drawback by deliberately over-invoicing the readymade garments. The Commissioner of Customs imposed a redemption fine of Rs. 10,00,000/- and levied a penalty of Rs. 20,00,000/-. It was held that no drawback was admissible even if the party exported the goods in terms of Section 76 of the Act as the market value of the goods was less than the amount of drawback claimed.

2. Being aggrieved by the said order, the appellant filed appeal before the Customs, Excise and Gold (Control) Appellate Tribunal, New Delhi (hereinafter referred to as 'the Tribunal'). The Tribunal also dismissed the appeal and held that the over-invoicing of the goods for exportation was an offence under the Act. Hence, this appeal.

CHAPTER FOURTEEN

Commissioner of Customs, New Delhi vs. Punjab Stainless Steel Industries (31.07.2001 - SC) : MANU/SC/0402/2001

Relative Section:

Customs Act, 1962 - Section 113, Customs Act, 1962 - Section 114, Customs Act, 1962 - Section 130, Customs Act, 1962 - Section 130E; Foreign Trade Development And Regulation Act, 1992 - Section 11

Hon'bleJudges/Coram:

S.P. Bharucha, Y.K. Sabharwal and Brijesh Kumar, JJ.

Equivalent Citation: AIR2001SC3129, 2001(77)ECC6, 2001(97)ECR537(SC), 2001(132)ELT10(S.C.), JT2001(6)SC146, 2001(4)SCALE638, (2001)6SCC284

NumberofPagesintheOriginalJudgment: 4

Case Reference:

Commissioner of Central Excise & Customs v. Venus Castings (P) Ltd. MANU/SC/0239/2000; S.D. Kemexc Industries v. Collector of Central Excise, Calcutta MANU/CE/0522/1994; CCE v. Venus Castings P. Ltd. [(2000) 4 SCC 206];S.D. Kemexc Industries v. CCE [1995 (56) ECR 749 (T)]

Case Note:

Appeal filed under S. 130E of C.A. 1962 - Maintainability in view of the fact that the present case does not involve determination of any question relating to the rate of duty of Customs or to the value of goods for assessment--Appeal converted into special leave petition in view of the decision in the case CCE & C v. Venus Castings (P) Ltd. [(2000) 4 SCC 206].

Principles of natural justice--Violation--Request for retest and supply of shipping bill--Rejection of respondents' request for retest of the samples already tested by the Chemical Examiner and non-supply of shipping bills do not constitute violation of principles of natural justice--The idea of retest of samples was to demolish the test report of the Chemical Examiner. The respondent was given ample opportunity to cross-examine the Chemical Examiner. The respondent did not avail the opportunity on the misconceived and frivolous objection that the offer was made suo motu without the respondent asking for the same. The conclusion of the Tribunal regarding violation of principles of natural justice is thus not sustainable. The second conclusion of the Tribunal is also unsustainable because a copy of the test report establishing that inferior material has been used, had been supplied to the respondent. Therefore, non-supply of a copy of shipping bill to the respondent was of no consequence.

Limitation--Extended period--Erroneous conclusion of the Tribunal-- The conclusion of the Tribunal that extended period of limitation is not available to the appellant is erroneous because the charge of mis-statement and suppression against the respondent has been established. The reliance of the Tribunal on the Tribunal order in the case of S.D. Kemexc Industries v. CCE, Calcutta [1995 (56) ECR 749 (T)] is misplaced as misdeclaration and suppression had not been established and the demand was held to be time barred. Impugned Order of the Tribunal set aside.

Facts:

1. The respondent in discharge of its export obligation under quantity based advance licence, filed shipping bills for export of stainless steel utensils. One of the conditions of licence was that the utensils shall be made of AISI-202 quality stainless steels by using the raw material "non-magnetic stainless steel sheets/coils AISI-202 - indigenous" under proper declaration. The allegations against the respondent was that the goods exported under the export obligation were misdeclared inasmuch as the respondent had used the material of inferior grade to the one required in the manufacture of utensils. The Commissioner of Customs came to the conclusion that the charge against the respondent had been proved. The Commissioner for his

conclusion relied upon the report of the Chemical Examiner. The demand of the respondent for retesting of samples was declined but in order to obviate any unfair treatment to the respondent the Commissioner gave option to the respondent to cross-examine the Chemical Examiner who had tested the samples. The respondent, however, did not avail that option and declined to cross examine the Chemical Examiner. Regarding the objection of the respondent that copies of shipping bills were not supplied, the Commissioner observed that so long as report of the test conduct don the sample drawn from the respective consignments establishing that the grade of material used in the utensils exported under these consignments was substandard, was supplied to the respondent, it was immaterial whether copy of the shipping bills was supplied or not. After detailed examination of the record, the Commissioner held that the charge of mis-statement and suppressing the correct quality and grade of the input under claim of duty exemption entitlement under quantity based advance licence and DEEC Book in violation of the standard input-output value addition norms mentioned therein stood established in respect of 67 out of 88 consignments. The Commissioner of Customs by order dated 3rd November, 1997, held that the goods amounting to Rs.6,74,43,408/- are liable to confiscation under Section 113(n) and (j) of the Customs Act, 1962(for short, `the Act'). Further, the bank guarantee of Rs.10,00,000/- was ordered to be appropriated against the liability of confiscation as the goods had already been exported. The respondent was also denied the benefit of the amount of Rs.4,68,78,932/- under DEEC Scheme and duty drawback in respect of these consignments directing that if these concessions have already availed by the respondent, the same shall be revered. Further, a penalty of Rs.25,00,000/- was imposed on the respondent under Section 114 of the Acts read with Section 11 of the Foreign Trade(Development and Regulation) Act, 1962.

Held, while allowing the appeal:

4. The order of the Commissioner of Customs has been set aside by the Tribunal holding that there was violation of principles of natural justice on account of two reasons, namely, (1) Rejection of the request of the respondent for retesting the samples on the ground that there is no such provision in the Act and (2) Non-supply of the copy of the shipping bills.

5. Regarding the first reason, noticing the contention urged on behalf of the Revenue that three is no provision which persist retesting of sample the Tribunal states that there is also no provision under the Customs Act

which prohibits retesting of the samples, and accordingly holding that the denial of opportunity to retest the sample was violative of principles of natural justice. No specific provision has been brought to our notice which permits retesting of samples, but, for the present case, without going into that aspect, we would assume that there was no bar in granting opportunity to retest the samples. At the same time, however, it had to be born in mind that the purpose of retesting the samples was to demolish the report of the Chemical Examiner on consideration whereof the charge of mis-statement and suppression regarding quality and grade of the input had been established against the respondent. In this regard, the Tribunal failed to notice the main aspect of the case that option was granted to the respondent to cross-examine the Chemical Examiner who after taking the samples had given the report. The respondent had, thus, ample opportunity to demolish his report. The respondent did not avail that appertained. It stands establish that the adjudicating officer had given an offer to the respondent to cross-examine the Chemical Examiner. The respondent did not dispute that such an offer was made. The only objection of the respondent was that such an offer was made suo moto and the respondent had not asked for it. The objection was frivolous and misconceived. Therefore, we fail to understand, how the respondent having failed to availed the opportunity to cross-examine the Chemical Examiner could urge that there was violation of principles of natural justice by non-grant of request of the respondent for retesting of the samples. Unfortunately, in the order of the Tribunal there is not even a whisper about the offer given to the respondent to cross-examine the Chemical Examiner. Thus, the first reason given by the Tribunal for coming to the conclusion that there has been violation of the principles of natural justice ins not sustainable.

6. The second reason given by the Tribunal is also unsustainable as the non-supply of copy of the shipping bills containing the examination report was of no consequence as admittedly the rapport of the test conducted on the samples drawn on the respective consignments establishing that the inferior material has been used had been supplied to the respondent. Under these circumstances the reasoning of the Commissioner of Customs could not be faulted. Therefore, the conclusion of the Tribunal that the order passed by the Commissioner of Customs was a violation of principles of natural justice is unsustainable.

7. The Tribunal also held that the demand in respect of consignments was time barred as the test report was received by the revenue 6 months

before issue of show cause notice. In view of the finding that the charge of mis-statement of suppressing the correct quality has been established against the respondent, the demand cannot be held to be time barred. The conclusion of the Tribunal that the extended period of limitation is not available to the appellant is clearly erroneous. The reliance by the Tribunal on the order of Tribunal in the case of S.D. Kemexc Industries v. Collector of Central Excise, Calcutta MANU/CE/0522/1994 was also misplaced as in that case, the mis-declaration and suppression had not been established and, therefore, it was held that the demand was time barred. Clearly, therefore, the said decision had no applicability to the facts and circumstances of the present case.

8. For the aforesaid reasons we set aside the order of the Tribunal and restore the order of the Commissioner of Customs. The appeal is accordingly allowed with costs.

CHAPTER FIFTEEN

Dewan Tyres Ltd. vs. Union of India (24.04.2014 – ALLHC) : MANU/UP/1698/2014

Relative Section:

Andhra Pradesh (telangana Area) Tenancy And Agricultural Lands Act, 1950 - Section 50B; Central Excise Act, 1944 - Section 11AC; Constitution Of India - Article 14, Constitution Of India - Article 226; Customs Act, 1962 - Section 116; Foreign Trade Development And Regulation Act, 1992 - Section 11, Foreign Trade Development And Regulation Act, 1992 - Section 11(1), Foreign Trade Development And Regulation Act, 1992 - Section 11(2), Foreign Trade Development And Regulation Act, 1992 - Section 11(a), Foreign Trade Development And Regulation Act, 1992 - Section 12, Foreign Trade Development And Regulation Act, 1992 - Section 13, Foreign Trade Development And Regulation Act, 1992 - Section 14, Foreign Trade Development And Regulation Act, 1992 - Section 18, Foreign Trade Development And Regulation Act, 1992 - Section 19, Foreign Trade Development And Regulation Act, 1992 - Section 2(g), Foreign Trade Development And Regulation Act, 1992 - Section 20, Foreign Trade Development And Regulation Act, 1992 - Section 3, Foreign Trade Development And Regulation Act, 1992 - Section 8, Foreign Trade Development And Regulation Act, 1992 - Section 9; Himachal Pradesh Ceiling On Land Holdings Act, 1972 - Section 20, Himachal Pradesh Ceiling On Land Holdings Act, 1972 - Section 20(2)

Hon'bleJudges/Coram:

Sudhir Agarwal, J.

Equivalent Citation: 2014(307)ELT496(All.)

NumberofPagesintheOriginalJudgment: 14

Case Reference:

Neeldhara Weav. Factory vs. Dir. Gen. of Foreign Trade MANU/PH/ 1254/2006; Government of India vs. Citedal Fine Pharmaceuticals, Madras and Ors. MANU/SC/0198/1989; The State of Gujarat vs. Patil Raghav Natha and Ors. MANU/SC/0406/1969; Ibrahimpatnam Taluk Vyavasaya Collie Sangham vs. K. Suresh Reddy and Ors. MANU/SC/0616/2003; State of H.P. and Ors. vs. Rajkumar Brijender Singh and Ors. MANU/SC/0509/ 2004; Parekh Shipping Corporation vs. Asstt. Collector of Cus., Bombay MANU/MH/0224/1995; Wilco & Company, Madras vs. Union of India (UOI), represented by the Secretary, Ministry of Finance, Department of Revenue, Sansad Marg, New Delhi, MANU/TN/1633/2002; D. Saibaba vs. Bar Council of India and Anr. MANU/SC/0388/2003; Commnr. of Central Excise, Chandigarh vs. Pepsi Foods Ltd. MANU/SC/1049/2010

Case Note:

Excise - Imposition of penalty - Validity thereof - Section 11(a) of Foreign Trade (Development and Regulation) Act, 1992 - Present appeal filed for challenging order whereby, penalty was imposed under Section 11(a) of Act on ground of violation of provisions of Act - Whether penalty was rightly imposed upon Appellant - Held, Petitioners contented that Deputy Director General had not power to impose penalty - Held, Central Government had authorized various officers to function as adjudicating authorities competent to impose penalty under Section 11 of Act with reference to value of goods in respect of which power has to be exercised - Deputy Director General was well within his competence to take action under Section 11 of Act and pass order of penalty - Petitioners contended that there was no motive for violation of provisions of Act - It is penal provision empowering Authority to impose penalty on account of certain violation on part of Petitioners which was subject to imposition of penalty under statute - Perusal of orders showed that this aspect had been taken care by Authorities concerned before passing impugned orders - Petitioners contended that notice was not issued them - Court found that no valid notice had been issued to Petitioners - During course of argument counsel for Respondents admitted that copy of notice which they had filed showed that it was incomplete and misprinted notice form - Thus, notice could not be said to be valid notice issued to Petitioners and in absence of any valid notice order of penalty could not be sustained - Therefore, order of penalty was quashed - Petition allowed. [paras 26, 28, 50, 51 and 52]

Facts:

Petitioners were engaged in manufacturing of Automobile Tyres and Tubes. Petitioners had to import and export product. Petitioners had not furnished export details and thus, violated provisions of Foreign Trade (Development and Regulation) Act, 1992. Penalty was imposed upon Petitioners under Section 11(a) of Act. Hence, present petition.

Held:

Validity of imposition of penalty:

(i) Central Government had authorized various officers to function as adjudicating authorities competent to impose penalty under Section 11 of Act with reference to value of goods in respect of which power has to be exercised. [para 26]

Deputy Director General was well within his competence to take action under Section 11 of Act and pass order of penalty. [para 28]

(ii) Petitioners contended that there was no motive for violation of provisions of Act. [para 50]

(iii) It is penal provision empowering Authority to impose penalty on account of certain violation on part of Petitioners which was subject to imposition of penalty under statute. Perusal of orders showed that this aspect had been taken care by Authorities concerned before passing impugned orders.[para 51]

(iv) Petitioners contended that notice was not issued them. Court found that no valid notice had been issued to Petitioners. During course of argument counsel for Respondents admitted that copy of notice which they had filed showed that it was incomplete and misprinted notice form. Thus, notice could not be said to be valid notice issued to Petitioners and in absence of any valid notice order of penalty could not be sustained. Therefore, order of penalty was quashed. [para 52]

CHAPTER SIXTEEN

Doab Exim (P.) Ltd. and Ors. vs. Addl. Director General, Foreign Trade and Ors. (16.05.2016 – ALLHC) : MANU/UP/1901/2016

Relative Section:

Foreign Trade Development And Regulation Act, 1992 - Section 11(2), Foreign Trade Development And Regulation Act, 1992 - Section 15, Foreign Trade Development And Regulation Act, 1992 - Section 16

Hon'bleJudges/Coram:

Pankaj Mithal, J.

Equivalent Citation: 2016(9)ADJ270, 2016 (118) ALR 61, 2016 5 AWC4864All

NumberofPagesintheOriginalJudgment: 2

Case Reference: nil

Case Note:

Foreign Trade (Development and Regulation) Act, 1992 - Sections 11 (2), 15 and 16--Constitution of India--Article 226--Fiscal penalty -- For non-fulfilment of export obligation and violation of condition of authorisation--Dismissal of appeal against -- Writ petition-- Maintainability of--Petitioner had statutory alternate remedy of getting appellate order revised by Central Government/Director General--Hence, held that they were not entitled to invoke powers and approach High Court straightway for exercise of extra-ordinary jurisdiction--Writ petition dismissed on ground of alternate remedy. [2], [4], [5], [8] and [9]

Facts:

The petitioners have preferred this writ petition against the order dated 11.5.2011 passed by the Foreign Trade Development Officer and the order dated 30.4.2015 passed by the Additional Director General of Foreign Trade, dismissing the appeal thereto.

The adjudicating authority under the Foreign Trade (Development and Regulation) Act, 1992 on 11.5.2011 passed an order imposing a fiscal penalty of ` 2,03,17,600/- (Rupees two crore three lakh seventeen thousand and six hundred only) upon the petitioner for non-fulfillment of the export obligation and violation of the condition of the authorization in exercise of the powers under section 11(2) of the Act. The petitioner preferred an appeal against the aforesaid order under section 15 of the Act which has also been dismissed vide order dated 30.4.2015.

Section 16 of the Act provides for the review of the orders passed by the subordinate authority by Central Government or the Director General. It lays down that the Central Government in case of any decision or order made by the Director General, or the Director General in the case of any decision made by any other officer subordinate to him, may on his own motion or otherwise, call for the records and examine the correctness and legality or propriety of any such decision subject to certain conditions.

Held, while allowing the appeal:

The aforesaid power conferred upon the Central Government or the Director General is akin to the power of revision which is generally conferred upon the higher authority.

1. The aforesaid power given under section 16 of the Act is primarily that of revision of the orders of the subordinate authorities by the Central Government or the Director General and not actually the power to review which is vested not in the higher/superior authority but upon the same authority passing the order. Therefore, the power of review mentioned in section 16 of the Act has to be read as that of revision.[6]

2. In view of the above, the petitioners have statutory remedy of getting the appellate order revised by the Central Government/Director General as the case may be. Accordingly when the petitioners have a statutory remedy available to them they are not entitle to invoke the constitutional powers and to approach this Court straight-way for exercise of extra ordinary jurisdiction.[7]

3. The writ petition is dismissed on the ground of alternate remedy. Certified copy of the impugned orders enclosed with the writ petition are directed to be returned to Sri Vikrant Rana, learned Counsel for the petitioners after retaining photocopies of the same on record.[8]

CHAPTER SEVENTEEN

Jagdish Singh vs. State of Rajasthan (20.05.2016 - RAJHC) : MANU/RH/1272/2016

Relative Section:

Atomic Energy Act, 1962 - Section 14, Atomic Energy Act, 1962 - Section 2, Atomic Energy Act, 1962 - Section 2(1)(g), Atomic Energy Act, 1962 - Section 24, Atomic Energy Act, 1962 - Section 3; Code of Criminal Procedure, 1973 (CrPC) - Section 41; Code of Criminal Procedure, 1973 (CrPC) - Section 439; Foreign Trade Development And Regulation Act, 1992 - Section 14A, Foreign Trade Development And Regulation Act, 1992 - Section 5; Indian Penal Code 1860, (IPC) - Section 379; National Investigation Agency Act 2008 - Section 20, National Investigation Agency Act 2008 - Section 21(1), National Investigation Agency Act 2008 - Section 21(4), National Investigation Agency Act 2008 - Section 22(1), National Investigation Agency Act 2008 - Section 22(3), National Investigation Agency Act 2008 - Section 6(1), National Investigation Agency Act 2008 - Section 6(2), National Investigation Agency Act 2008 - Section 6(3), National Investigation Agency Act 2008 - Section 6(5), National Investigation Agency Act 2008 - Section 6(7); Prevention Of Damage To Public Property Act, 1984 - Section 3

Hon'bleJudges/Coram:
Mohammad Rafiq and Vijay Kumar Vyas, JJ.
Equivalent Citation: 2016(4)RLW3464(Raj.)
NumberofPagesintheOriginalJudgment: 5

Case Reference:

Bahadur Kora and Ors. vs. The State of Bihar MANU/BH/0261/2015;
Arnesh Kumar vs. State of Bihar MANU /SC/0559/2014

Case Note:

National Investigation Agency Act, 2008, Sec. 21(4); Atomic Energy Act, 1962, Sec. 14/24; I.P.C., Sec. 379; Prevention of Damage to Public Property Act, 1984, Sec. 3, Cr.P.C., 1973, Sec. 439 - Appeal against rejection of bail - Found in possession of 10 tonnes of beryl ore, a "prescribed substance" - Challan filed and charges framed - In jail for 4-1/2 months - Held - The number of prosecution witnesses being 59, the trial is likely to take a long time - Enlarged on bail on furnishing bail bonds of Rs. 2 lac with two sureties each of Rs. 1 lac - Left it open to the appellant to raise objection with regard to competence and jurisdiction before the Court of sessions concerned. [11] to [13]

Facts:

This appeal under Section 21(4) of the National Investigation Agency Act, 2008, has been filed by appellant Jagdish Singh challenging order dated 21.01.2016 passed by learned Sessions Judge, Jaipur Metropolitan, Jaipur, by which his application for grant of bail under Sec. 439 of the Code of Criminal Procedure (for short, 'the Cr.P.C.'), has been rejected. Accused-appellant was arrested in connection with investigation of F.I.R. No. 10/ 2015 registered against him and certain other accused on 30.12.2015 with Police Station C.I.D., Jaipur, for offence under Section 14/24 of the Atomic Energy Act, 1962, Section 379 of the Indian Penal Code and Section 3 of the Prevention of Damage to Public Property Act, 1984 (for short, 'the PDPP Act'). The F.I.R. was registered on the basis of a complaint submitted by Mr. Rama Kant Purohit, Regional Director of Atomic Minerals Directorate for Exploration and Research, Department of Atomic Energy, Jaipur. Allegation against appellant is that he was found in possession of large quantity of beryl ore, which, according to the Notification dated 18.01.2006 issued by the Atomic Energy Department, Mumbai, under Clauses (f) and (g) of sub-sec. (1) of Sec. 2 and Sec. 3 of the Atomic Energy Act, 1962, in supersession of earlier Notification dated 15.03.1995 published in the Gazette Extra Ordinary dated 20.01.2006, is a 'Prescribed Substance'. His act, therefore, constituted an offence u/Sec. 14 of the Atomic Energy Act, 1962 (for short, 'the Act of 1962').

Held, while allowing the appeal:

1. Having regard to rival submissions and taking into consideration the fact that accused-appellant has been in jail since 06.01.2016 and the maximum sentence that can be awarded for scheduled offence under Section 14/24 is for a term which can be extended up to five years or fine alone can be awarded as sentence and also for offence under Section 379 of the IPC and the maximum sentence awardable is for the term which may extend to three years, which may also be punished with fine alone, and offence under Section 3 of the PDPP Act may be punished with maximum sentence of five years and fine, and taking into consideration the fact that number of prosecution witnesses being 59, the trial is likely to take a long, we are inclined to enlarge the appellant on bail on his furnishing bail bonds of Rs. 2,00,000/- with two sureties, each of Rs. 1,00,000/- to the satisfaction of the court concerned.[10]

2. We are, however, for the present, not dealing with the question of jurisdiction and competence of the court of Sessions to try the present matter in view of what has been provided in Section 20 of the NIA Act, which stipulates that even after taking cognizance of any offence, if a special court is of the opinion that offence is not triable by it, it shall, notwithstanding that it has no jurisdiction to try such offence, transfer the case for the trial of such offence to the court having jurisdiction under the Code of Criminal Procedure and the court, to which the case is transferred, may proceed with the trial of offence as if it has taken cognizance of the offence. That course of action appears more appropriate to us because in Bahadur Kora, supra, the judgment rendered by Full Bench of Patna High Court, investigation in all cases before that court was originally conducted by the agencies of the State Government, which filed the charge sheet in the courts of competent jurisdiction as per the provisions of Cr.P.C. Eventually all such cases were transferred to the Special Courts pursuant to interpretation placed on the provisions of N.I.A. Act by Division Bench of Patna High Court in Asif P.K. v. State of Bihar - (2015) 1 DLJR 1015, which interpretation the learned Additional Advocate General would commend us to adopt in the present case. It was in those facts that the Patna High Court directed restoration of all such cases to the courts that otherwise have jurisdiction to try them. There was therefore no occasion for the Special Courts in those cases to examine such objection with regard to its jurisdiction under Section 20 of the NIA Act. We therefore leave it open to the appellant to raise such objection with regard to competence and jurisdiction before the Court of Sessions concerned. If any such objection

is raised, the said court shall expeditiously decide the same in accordance with the law.[11]

CHAPTER EIGHTEEN

Hubergroup India Private Limted vs. Union of India (21.08.2019 - GUJHC) : MANU/GJ/1650/2019

Relative Section:

Central Excise Act, 1944 (repealed) - Section 3, Central Excise Act, 1944 (repealed) - Section 37; Constitution Of India - Article 226, Constitution Of India - Article 246, Constitution Of India - Article 265; Customs Act, 1962 - Section 75; Finance Act, 1994 - Section 93A, Finance Act, 1994 - Section 94; Foreign Trade (development And Regulation) Act, 1992 - Section 11, Foreign Trade (development And Regulation) Act, 1992 - Section 13, Foreign Trade (development And Regulation) Act, 1992 - Section 14D, Foreign Trade (development And Regulation) Act, 1992 - Section 15, Foreign Trade (development And Regulation) Act, 1992 - Section 16, Foreign Trade (development And Regulation) Act, 1992 - Section 19, Foreign Trade (development And Regulation) Act, 1992 - Section 3, Foreign Trade (development And Regulation) Act, 1992 - Section 5, Foreign Trade (development And Regulation) Act, 1992 - Section 6, Foreign Trade (development And Regulation) Act, 1992 - Section 6(3), Foreign Trade (development And Regulation) Act, 1992 - Section 8, Foreign Trade (development And Regulation) Act, 1992 - Section 9

Hon'bleJudges/Coram:

J.B. Pardiwala and A.C. Rao, JJ.

Equivalent Citation: C/SCA/1849/2019

NumberofPagesintheOriginalJudgment: 16

Case Reference:

Asahi Songwon Colors Ltd. and Ors. vs. Union of India and Ors. MANU/
GJ/1162/2017; Alstom India Ltd. vs. Union of India MANU/GJ/0210/2014;
Hospira Health Care India Pvt. Ltd. vs. Development Commissioner, MEPZ
Special Economic Zone and HEOUs and Ors. MANU/TN/1057/2016

Case Note:

Sales Tax / VAT - Refund - Provisions of Foreign Trade Policy - Present
petition filed for quashing impugned order holding that said order is
arbitrary, issued in violation of principles of natural justice, non-speaking,
vague, omits relevant provisions of Foreign Trade Policy (FTP), going
beyond FTP, discriminatory, time barred - Whether order impugned herein
calls for interference - Held, provisions in FTP govern statutory scheme
of policy - Appendix or Handbook of Procedures cannot override FTP
provisions - In case of conflict, FTP provisions should prevail vis-a-vis
appendix in Handbook of Procedure - Policy making authority never invited
to distinguish raw materials used for production of goods cleared into DTA
vis-a-vis raw materials used in final product used for other clearance for
grant of refund of CST products on same raw materials - Impugned order
arbitrary and set aside - Petition allowed. [22]

Facts:

1. By this writ application under Article 226 of the Constitution of India,
the writ applicant has prayed for the following reliefs:

"A. Your Lordships be pleased to issue a writ of mandamus or in the
nature of mandamus or certiorari or any other appropriate writ quashing
the impugned order dated 07.09.2018 in Annexure-A hereto holding that
the impugned order in Annexure-A is arbitrary, issued in violation of the
principles of natural justice, non-speaking, vague, omits relevant provisions
of the FTP, going beyond the FTP, discriminatory, time barred and therefore
illegal with consequential relief to petitioner company herein.

B. Your Lordships be pleased to hold that CST refunds granted to
petitioner company's EOU (1) in respect of inputs procured from other
EOUs and (2) in respect of inputs used in production of final products
cleared into DTA are in order and in accordance with Exim Policy 2004-09.

C. Your Lordships be pleased to hold that Public Notice No. 81
(RE-2008)/2004-2009 dated 16.09.2008 amending Appendix 14-1 of
Handbook of Procedures is only clarificatory as it only accords with them
existing paragraph 6.11 (c) of Exim Policy 2004-2009.

D. Pending hearing and final disposal of this Special Civil Application, ad-interim order staying the operation of the impugned order at Annexure-A with a direction to respondent NO. 3 Development Commissioner and officers under him not to initiate any recovery proceedings against the petitioner may kindly be granted.

E. As ex-parte ad interim relief in terms of prayer (D) above may kindly be granted; and

F. Such other and further or incidental reliefs as may be deemed just and proper in the fats and circumstances of the present case may kindly be granted."

Held, while allowing the appeal:

1. We find merit in the submission of Mr. Iyer that the provisions in the FTP govern the statutory scheme of the policy, and in such circumstances, the appendix or the Handbook of Procedures cannot override the FTP provisions. In case of a conflict, the FTP provisions should prevail vis-a-vis the appendix in Handbook of Procedures, which are nothing but a subordinate legislation. It was also pointed out by Mr. Iyer that in the appendix 14 I-I of the Handbook of Procedures, the following condition existed:[22]

"(a) The goods for which the claim has been made are meant for utilization/production of goods/services of the EOU/EHTP/STP unit and will be utilised only in our factory and we shall not divert or dispose off the material procured without obtaining prior permission of the concerned Development Commissioner."

2. Relying on the aforesaid, it is submitted that the policy making authority never invited to distinguish the raw materials used for the production of goods cleared into the DTA vis-a-vis the raw materials used in the final product used for other clearance for the grant of refund of the CST products on the same raw materials.[23]

3. For the foregoing reasons, this petition succeeds and is hereby allowed. The impugned order passed by the Director General of Foreign Trade dated 7th September 2018 is hereby quashed and set aside. Rule is made absolute.[24]

CHAPTER NINETEEN

Taarika Exports and Ors. vs. Union of India (UOI) and Ors. (07.05.2007 - SC) : MANU/ SC/7621/2007

Relative Section:

Constitution Of India - Article 226; Foreign Trade Development And Regulation Act, 1992 - Section 20(2); Imports And Exports (control) Act, 1947 [repealed] - Section 4-I(1), Imports And Exports (control) Act, 1947 [repealed] - Section 4I, Imports And Exports (control) Act, 1947 [repealed] - Section 4L

Hon'bleJudges/Coram:

Dr. Arijit Pasayat and Devinder Kumar Jain, JJ.

Equivalent Citation: AIR2007SC1844, 2007(6)ALT25(SC), 2007(212)ELT15(S.C.), JT2007(6)SC569, 2007(6)SCALE548, (2007)5SCC254, [2007]7SCR94

NumberofPagesintheOriginalJudgment:5

Case Reference:nil

Case Note:

Export and Import - Penalty -Violation of conditions of advance licence-Section 4-I of Import (Control) Order, 1955 and Foreign Trade (Development and Regulation) Act, 1992 - Appellant was engaged in export and import activities - Advance licence was issued to appellant for import and export - Appellant used the licence in full so far as the import of raw materials but only exported a part of finished goods under the said license - Show cause notice issued to appellant and a penalty was imposed for not fulfilling export obligation - Appeal dismissed by High Court - Hence, present appeal - Appellant contended that conditions were incapable of compliance - Held, the plea that the conditions were incapable of compliance is in variance with the stand taken earlier - earlier appellants made a request to the Regional Licensing Authority for grant of extension of six months to enable them to comply with the export obligations - Plea rightly turned down by authorities and High Court - Penalty reduced from Rs. 45 lakhs to Rs. 20 lakhs

Ratio Decidendi : Penalty -Violation of conditions of advance licence - Quantum of

Facts:

1. A show cause notice was issued to the appellants under Section 4L of the Imports and Exports (Control) Act, 1947 (in short the 'Act') for action under Section 4I and under Clause 10 for action under Clause 8 of the Import (Control) Order, 1955 (in short 'Control Order") read with Section 20(2) of the Foreign Trade (Development and Regulation) Act, 1992 (in short "Foreign Trade Act") for not exporting the goods as also utilizing the imported goods and failure to export within the stipulated time. The appellants during the material point of time were engaged in the import and export activities under the Import and Export Code. On 13.10.1991 the Regional Licensing Authority had issued an advance licence to the appellants. The appellants undisputedly used the license in full so far as the import of raw materials thereunder free of customs duty is concerned but only a part of the finished goods under the said licence was exported. Resultantly, there was a shortfall on account of export obligation. Appellants submitted that the conditions under the licence were unrealistic and, therefore, non-fulfillment of the obligation was beyond their control. The show cause notice in question was issued on 7.5.1995 proposing, inter alia, imposition of fiscal penalty for non fulfillment of export obligation under the licence as well as for mis-utilization of the goods valued at Rs. 9,10,125/- imported under the said licence free of customs duty. Appellants submitted their reply to the show cause notice. The Additional Director General of Foreign Trade (in short 'DGFT') passed an order dated 13.11.1995 imposing a penalty of Rs. 45 lakhs for shortfall in export obligation to the extent of Rs. 27,20,462/-. An appeal was preferred before the Appellate Committee. By order dated 12.8.1997 the Appellate Committee dismissed the appeal of the appellants. Subsequently, a writ petition was filed under Article 226 of the Constitution of India, 1950 (in

short the 'Constitution') before the Delhi High Court. The writ petition was numbered as CWP. 623 of 1998. By judgment and order dated 30.5.2003 learned Single Judge dismissed the writ petition holding that there was no ground to interfere with the orders of the adjudicating authority as well as the Appellate Committee. A Letters Patent Appeal was filed which as noted above was dismissed by a Division Bench.[4]

Held, while allowing the appeal:

1. The stand that the conditions were incapable of compliance seems to be at variance with the stand taken earlier. By letter dated 22.12.1992 appellants made a request to the Regional Licensing Authority for grant of extension of six months to enable them to export the balance quantity by 30.4.1993. They again applied to the Joint Director General of Foreign Trade, Bombay Office for further extension. The same was rejected. Period of export obligation expired on 30.4.1993. Subsequently, the appellants approached DGFT office several times for extension of export obligation period which was rejected. Therefore, the plea that the conditions were incapable of compliance has been rightly turned down by the authorities and the High Court.[11]

2. Finally, it was submitted that considering the value of the articles involved, imposition of penalty of Rs. 45 lakhs is extremely high. The minimum penalty provided is Rs. 1,000/-and the maximum is five times of the value of goods involved.[12]

3. Considering the value of the articles involved we are of the view that penalty of Rs. 20 lakhs instead of Rs. 45 lakhs would meet the ends of justice. It is submitted that pursuant to the order of this Court dated 9.12.2005 a sum of Rs. 20 lakhs had been deposited by the appellants. If that is so, there shall not be requirement of making any further deposit.[13]

4. The appeal is disposed of accordingly with no order as to costs. [14]

CHAPTER TWENTY

Union of India (UOI) and Ors. vs. T.R. Mehra and Ors. (21.08.2019 – SC) : MANU/ SC/1208/2019

Relative Section:

Foreign Trade (Development and Regulation) Act, 1992 - Section 20, Foreign Trade (Development and Regulation) Act, 1992 - Section 20(2), Foreign Trade (Development and Regulation) Act, 1992 - Section 20(3); Foreign Trade (Development and Regulation) Ordinance, 1992; General Clauses Act; Imports and Exports (Control) Act, 1947

Hon'bleJudges/Coram:

A.M. Khanwilkar and Dinesh Maheshwari, JJ.

Equivalent Citation: 2020(208)AIC197, 2020 (140) ALR 776, 2019(368)ELT11(S.C.), 2019/ INSC 929, 2019(12)SCALE164, (2020)15SCC125, [2019]11SCR278

NumberofPagesintheOriginalJudgment:2

Case Reference: nil

Case Note:

INDIRECT TAXES MATTERS : IMPORT CONTROL ORDER - the Act provides for a savings Clause to save the quasi judicial order passed by the Competent Authority in exercise of powers bestowed in it in terms of Imports (Control) Order, 1986.- The provisions of the Act as rightly noted by the High Court, in no manner save the quasi judicial order.- it had the effect of continuing prohibition regarding the import of goods otherwise made free and could be imported under the 1992 Act. Any other interpretation would result in validating the quasi judicial order issued in exercise of powers derived from the Statutory Order which itself stands repealed alongwith the repealed Act. In other words, the quasi judicial order dated 14.11.1986 is repugnant to the legislative intent behind the 1992 Act, whereby, import in respect of the stated goods has been made free and an open regime.

1. A fortiori, no action against the Respondents in relation to import of stated goods after coming into force of the 1992 Act with effect from 17.08.1992, in reference to the order dated 14.11.1986 could be resorted to in law. The High Court has dealt with this contention exhaustively and, in our opinion, justly concluded that the show cause notice issued against the Respondents on the basis of order passed by the Competent Authority dated 14.11.1986 cannot stand the test of judicial scrutiny.[5]

2. Learned Counsel for the Appellants invited our attention to Section 20 of the Foreign Trade (Development and Regulation) Act, 1992.

Facts:

1. The action taken against the Respondents was founded on order dated 14.11.1986 passed by the Competent Authority in exercise of powers conferred by Clause 8(1) of the Imports (Control) Order, 1986 qua M/s. L.D. Textile Industries Ltd.[2]

2. It is not in dispute that the import of goods by Obron Impex (Pvt.) Ltd. was in August, 1997. After coming into force of the Foreign Trade (Development and Regulation) Act, 1992 (hereinafter referred to as the 'Act'), indisputably, import of stated goods is in no way prohibited under that Act. [3]

Held, while allowing the appeal:

1. However, the Appellants are not in a position to point out as to how the subject order dated 14.11.1986 would be covered by the savings Clause Under Sub-sections (2) or (3) of the Section 20 of the Act. Even the saving provision under the General Clauses Act will be of no avail to the Appellants for the reasons mentioned hitherto.[7]

2. In view of the above, no interference is required. For, a quasi judicial order passed in exercise of powers under the Statutory Order which stands repealed along with the repealed Act, is not saved especially when it will be per se repugnant to 1992 Act and defeat the spirit of opening of the import regime for the stated goods.[8]

3. Hence, these appeals must fail and the same are dismissed accordingly.

4. Pending applications, if any, stand disposed of.

CHAPTER TWENTY-ONE

Jaymatajee Enterprise (Seller) and Ors. vs. Commissioner of Customs (Preventive) and Ors. (22.10.2020 - ALLHC) : MANU/UP/2180/2020

Relative Section:

Constitution Of India - Article 226; Customs Act, 1962 - Section 108, Customs Act, 1962 - Section 109, Customs Act, 1962 - Section 110, Customs Act, 1962 - Section 110(1), Customs Act, 1962 - Section 110-A, Customs Act, 1962 - Section 110A, Customs Act, 1962 - Section 111, Customs Act, 1962 - Section 123, Customs Act, 1962 - Section 125, Customs Act, 1962 - Section 14(2), Customs Act, 1962 - Section 144, Customs Act, 1962 - Section 151 A, Customs Act, 1962 - Section 151-A, Customs Act, 1962 - Section 32, Customs Act, 1962 - Section 33, Customs Act, 1962 - Section 34, Customs Act, 1962 - Section 45, Customs Act, 1962 - Section 54, Customs Act, 1962 - Section 7, Customs Act, 1962 - Section 77; Foreign Trade (development And Regulation) Act, 1992 - Section 11; Securitisation And Reconstruction Of Financial Assets And Enforcement Of Security Interest Act, 2002 - Section 13

Hon'bleJudges/Coram:

Shashi Kant Gupta and Pankaj Bhatia, JJ.

Equivalent Citation: 2020(10)ADJ530, 2020 5 AWC5075All, (2020)ILR 11All13

NumberofPagesintheOriginalJudgment:10
Case Reference:
State of Uttar Pradesh vs. Kay Pan Fragrance Pvt. Ltd. MANU/SC/1820/
2019
Case Note:
Customs Act, 1962 - Sections 110, 110A and 111--Seizure and confiscation of the seized goods--No appeal lies against a seizure order--Goods detained perishable--Seizure memo and provisional release order contrary to the Act and departmental instructions--Writ petition challenging the seizure order maintainable--Goods in question purchased in an E-auction held by the Customs authorities themselves within the Indian territory--Power of seizure of goods under Section 110 of the Customs Act can be resorted to only when the officer exercising power has reason to believe that goods are liable to confiscation--Nothing on record to form a belief that goods in question were imported without payment of duty--Transport documents reveal that goods were being transported within India--Prima facie "reason to believe" not sustainable--Seizure order being illegal quashed--Respondent authorities directed to release the seized goods as well as the vehicle in question in favour of petitioners--Writ petition allowed. [25], [26] and [35]

Facts:
The petitioners received an order from one M/s. Jagdamba Enterprises for supplying 17920 K.G. of betel nuts and the petitioner purchased 24,000 K.G. of betel nuts from one Neelkamal Saha, West Bengal by means of two tax invoices dated 14.8.2020 each for 12,000 K.G. It is also stated that said Neelkamal Saha had purchased 19,884 K.G. of betel nuts in an E-auction held by the Customs Department. It is further stated that the petitioners and the purchaser Jagdamba Enterprises both are registered under the GS.T. Act. After purchasing the said betel nuts from the said Neelkamal Saha, the petitioners transported the said goods to the consignee M/s. Jagdamba Enterprises through Truck No. DL01 GC-1731 owned by the petitioner No. 2 and the goods were sent alongwith requisite E-Way Bill Invoices etc. It is further stated that the goods were valued for the total consignment value of Rs. 29,56,800/-. As soon as the Truck carrying the betel nuts entered the State of Uttar Pradesh, the respondent No. 3 intercepted the said Truck and vide Panchnama dated 17.8.2020, seized the goods as well as the vehicle i.e. Truck No. DL01 GC-1731. A copy of the Panchnama is on record as Annexure-3 to the writ petition.

Held, while allowing the appeal:

The petitioners received an order from one M/s. Jagdamba Enterprises for supplying 17920 K.G. of betel nuts and the petitioner purchased 24,000 K.G. of betel nuts from one Neelkamal Saha, West Bengal by means of two tax invoices dated 14.8.2020 each for 12,000 K.G. It is also stated that said Neelkamal Saha had purchased 19,884 K.G. of betel nuts in an E-auction held by the Customs Department. It is further stated that the petitioners and the purchaser Jagdamba Enterprises both are registered under the GS.T. Act. After purchasing the said betel nuts from the said Neelkamal Saha, the petitioners transported the said goods to the consignee M/s. Jagdamba Enterprises through Truck No. DL01 GC-1731 owned by the petitioner No. 2 and the goods were sent alongwith requisite E-Way Bill Invoices etc. It is further stated that the goods were valued for the total consignment value of Rs. 29,56,800/-. As soon as the Truck carrying the betel nuts entered the State of Uttar Pradesh, the respondent No. 3 intercepted the said Truck and vide Panchnama dated 17.8.2020, seized the goods as well as the vehicle i.e. Truck No. DL01 GC-1731. A copy of the Panchnama is on record as Annexure-3 to the writ petition.

Adv. Jayprakash Somani's Videos On Law

Adv. Jayprakash Somani's Videos on Law on Youtube- 'jaysomani64' channel.

1) SLP in Supreme Court / Special Leave Petitions in the Supreme Court of India

2) Transfer of Civil & Criminal Cases by the Supreme Court of India / Transfer of Matrimonial Cases

3) Appellate Jurisdiction of the Supreme Court of India

4) Jurisdictions of the Supreme Court of India

5) Public Interest Litigation in the Supreme Court of India / PIL in Supreme Court

6) Article 32 Writ Petitions in the Supreme Court of India

7) Bail Matters Top 10 Supreme Court Cases

8) FIR Quashing in High Court & Supreme Court

9) Bail & Anticipatory Bail Matters in Supreme Court

10) Insolvency & Bankruptcy Matters in the Supreme Court

11) Insolvency & Bankruptcy Code 2016 Part 1

12) Insolvency & Bankruptcy Code 2016 Part 2

13) Insolvency & Bankruptcy Code 2016 Part 3

14) Corporate Liquidation Process

15) Supreme Court Rules & Procedures Webinar of 2.5 hour on Zoom

16) RDDBFI Act, 1993 (Introduction)

17) The Indian Contact Act 1872

18) Negotiable Instruments Act (Introduction)

19) How to avoid matrimonial disputes& some more videos

20) SEBI Matters in the Supreme Court

21) Matrimonial Matters: Supreme Court's 20 Case Laws

22) Consumer Matters Supreme Court's 20 Case Laws

23) Service Matters Supreme Court's 20 Case Laws

24) How to Search Lawyer for Your Matter

25) Property Matters Supreme Court's 20 Case Laws

26) Bail Matters: Supreme Court's 20 Case Laws

27) Supreme Court / High Court Vacation Benches

28) 69000 Teacher's Recruitment Matters of UP Government in the Supreme Court

29) Contempt of Court Matters in the Supreme Court

30) Advocate Act's Matters in the Supreme Court

31) Business Law Matters in the Supreme Court

32) Banking Matters in the Supreme Court

33) Labour Law Matters in the Supreme Court

34) Arbitration Matters in the Supreme Court

35) Careers in Law -Zoom Webinar by Adv. Jayprakash Somani

36) Civil Matters in the Supreme Court

37) Consumer Protection Act | Consumer Matters in the Supreme Court

38) Corporate Matters in the Supreme Court

39) Criminal Matters in the Supreme Court

40) Role of Respondent in the Supreme Court of India

41) Motor Vehicle Accident Matters in Supreme Court with case laws

42) Article 131 Original Suits in Supreme Court

43) PIL in Supreme Court/ Public Interest Litigations in the Supreme Court of India'

44) CAB Citizenship Amendment Bill is not Unconstitutional

45) Supreme Court of India Cases & Process – Marathi

46) Legal Services Export / Export of Legal Services

47) Transfer of Matrimonial Cases by the Supreme Court of India

48) Public Interest Litigation PIL

49) The Specific Relief Act (Introduction)

50) Corporate Insolvency Resolution Process CIRP

51) ABMM's Career 5 - Careers in Law

52) Transfer of cases by Supreme Court

53) Writ Petitions in High Court & Supreme Court of India

54) Supreme Court Jurisdictions - Appeals, SLP, Writ Petitions, Transfer, Original, Review, Curative

55) LEGAL INDIA TV Show: Cases Handled in Supreme Court

56) Corporate Liquidation Process

57) Legal Services Export / Export of Legal Services

58) Corporate Laws

59) Election Matters- Supreme Court's 20 Case Laws

60) Companies Act, 2013

62) Competition Act, 2002

63) Banking Matters - Supreme Court's 20 Case Laws

64) Election Matters in the Supreme Court

65) Armed Forces Tribunal Matters in the Supreme Court

66) Compassionate Appointment Service matter

67) Foreign Exchange Management Act FEMA

68) Foreign Trade Policy 2021-26 Proposed

69) Customs Act 1962

70) Narcotic Drugs and Psychotropic Substances Act, 1985 NDPS Act

71) Foreign Trade Development & Regulation Act, 1992

72) How to Search Good Advocate in the Supreme Court of India

73) Sr. Adv Vikas Singh's Interview in Nani Palkhivala Wednesday Law Club

74) Indian Penal Code (I. P. C.)

75) Criminal Procedure Code (Cr. P. C.)

76) Commercial Courts & International Arbitration - by Mr. Jaideep Gupta, Senior Advocate in Nani Palkhivala Wednesday Law Club

77) Sr. Adv Ranji Thomos in Nani Palkhivala Wednesday Law Club

78) Urgent Matters in Supreme Court during vacations

79) 498A Bail Matters in Supreme Court

81) 376 Bail Matters in Supreme Court

82) 302, 304, 307, 308 Bail Matters in Supreme Court

83) 138, 420 Bail Matters in Supreme Court

84) POCSO Act Bail Matters in Supreme Court

85) NDPS Act Bail Matters in Supreme Court

86) What is ED (Enforcement Directorate)?

87) Prevention of Money Laundering Act, 2002 (PMLA Act)

88) Insolvency & Bankruptcy Code- Supreme Court Case Laws. Webinar in Nani Palkhivala Wednesday Law Club

89) What is NCLT & NCLAT?

90) Acquittal from 376- Supreme Court's some case laws in Nani Palkhivala Wednesday Law Club dt 28.7.22

91) Insolvency & Bankruptcy in India

92) Can we file case directly in the Supreme Court?

93) Adv. Anuja Pethia has cleared AOR Exam 2021 with 77% marks - Her interview in Nani Palkhivala Wednesday Law Club

94) Customs Act - Supreme Court Case Laws & Interview of AOR Adv. Anuja Pethia in Nani Palkhivala Law Club.

95) The Uttar Pradesh Public Service Tribunals Act, 1976

96) POCSO Act - Supreme Court Case Laws & Interview of AOR Adv. Shoumendu Mukharji & Adv. Nishant Verma in Nani Palkhivala Law Club.

97) Who Can Trigger CIRP Process Under Insolvency Law of India

98) The Uttar Pradesh Government Servant Discipline and Appeal Rules, 1999

99) CIRP Application Under Sec 7 by FC

100) Information Technology Act 2000

101) Uttar Pradesh Recruitment of Dependants of Government Servants Dying in Harness Rules, 1974

102) Foreign Exchange Management Act 1999 & Supreme Court's Case Laws on FEMA & Leading Case of AOR Exam in Nani Palkhivala Law Club.

103) Arbitration and Conciliation Act 1996 & It's Supreme Court Case Laws in Nani Palkhivala Wednesday Law Club.

104) Narcotic Drugs & Psychotropic Substances Act 1985 (NDPS Act) & It's Supreme Court Case Laws in Nani Palkhivala Wednesday Law Club.

105) Recovery of Debts and Bankruptcy Act 1993

106) Uttar Pradesh Land Revenue Code 2006

107) CIRP Application Under Sec 9 by OC

108) CIRP Application Under Sec 10 by CD

109) Hindu Succession Act, 1956

110) Maharashtra Civil Services Rules, 1981

111) Indian Contract Act, 1872 & Supreme Court's Case Laws" in Nani Palkhiwala Wednesday Law Club

112) Securities and Exchange Board of India Act, 1992 i. e. SEBI Act 1992 & Case Laws on Insiders Trading" in Nani Palkhiwala Wednesday Law Club

113) Moratorium Under Section 14 of IBC, 2016

114) Hindu Marriage Act, 1955

115) Maharashtra Land Revenue Code, 1966

116) 64 Leading Cases of AOR Exam Session 1 :- Cases 1 to16 in Nani Palkhiwala Wednesday Law Club

117) 64 Leading Cases of AOR Exam Session 2: Cases 17 to 32 in Nani Palkhiwala Wednesday Law Club

118) 64 Leading Cases of AOR Examination Session 3: Cases 33 to 48 in Nani Palkhivala Wednesday Law Club

119) 64 Leading Cases of AOR Exam Session 4: Cases 49 to 64 in Nani Palkhivala Wednesday Law Club

120) Labour Laws of India: Part 1 - 4 New Labour Law Codes of India

121) New Labour Laws Part 2 The Code on Wages, 2019

122) New Labour Laws Part 3:- The Code on Social Security, 2020

123) Argue in English Fluently & Confidently - Two months online course.

124) SLP Admission in the Supreme Court. 2023 (Hindi)

125) Transfer of Petitions from the Supreme Court (Hindi)

126) Review Petition in the Supreme Court.(Hindi)

127) Recovery of debts from the Company (Hindi)

128) How to search 'Good Insolvency & Bankruptcy Consultant?' (HINDI)

129) Curative Petition in the Supreme Court

130) AFT Appeals in the Supreme Court (HINDI)

131) NCLAT's Appeals in the Supreme Court.

132) Transfer Petition: Which matters can we transfer?

133) SLP Types of SLP in the Supreme court of India (English).

134) Argue in English Fluently and Confidently in the High Court & Supreme Court'.

List Of Adv. Jayprakash Somani's Published Books

1. Supreme Court of India's Leading Case Laws on 'Insolvency & Bankruptcy Code 2016'
2. Bail Matters – Supreme Court's Latest Leading Case Laws
3. Arbitration Matters- Supreme Court's Latest Leading Case Laws
4. Property Matters - Supreme Court's Latest Leading Case Laws
5. Matrimonial Matters- Supreme Court's Latest Leading Case Laws
6. Election Matters- Supreme Court's Latest Leading Case Laws
7. SEBI Matters- Supreme Court's Latest Leading Case Laws
8. Banking Matters- Supreme Court's Latest Leading Case Laws
9. Service Matters- Supreme Court's Latest Leading Case Laws
10. Contempt of Court Matters- Supreme Court's Latest Leading Case Laws
11. Consumer Protection Matters- Supreme Court's Latest Leading Case Laws
12. Corporate Law- Supreme Court's Latest Leading Case Laws
13. Supreme Court's AOR Exam- Leading Cases
14. Armed Force Tribunal - Supreme Court's Latest Leading Case Laws
15. Acquittal From 376 - Supreme Court's Latest Leading Case Laws
16. Negotiable instrument – Supreme Court's Latest Leading Case Laws
17. Contract Act- Supreme Court's Latest Leading Case Laws
18. Insider trading- Supreme Court's Latest Leading Case Laws
19. Foreign Exchange and Management Act- Supreme Court's Latest Leading Case Laws
20. Income Tax Act- Supreme Court's Latest Leading Case Laws
21. Company Law- Supreme Court's Latest Leading Case Laws
22. Competition & Monopoly Matters- Supreme Court's Latest Leading Case Laws
23. Compassionate Appointment- Service Matters- Supreme Court's Latest Leading Case Laws
24. Compulsory Retirement- Service Matters- Supreme Court's Latest Leading Case Laws
25. Voluntary Retirement- Service Matters- Supreme Court's Latest Leading Case Laws
26. Removal/Dismissal/Termination from Service- Supreme Court's Latest Leading Case Laws

27. Seniority- Service Matter- Supreme Court's Latest Leading Case Laws

28. Promotion- Service Matter- Supreme Court's Latest Leading Case Laws

29. Equal Pay for Equal Work- Service Matter- Supreme Court's Latest Leading Case Laws

30. Condition of Service- Service Matter- Supreme Court's Latest Leading Case Laws

31. Customs Act- Supreme Court's Leading Case Laws

32. Information Technology Act- Supreme Court's Leading Case Laws

33. SEC. 125 CR. P. C.- Supreme Court's Leading Case Laws

34. SEC. 498A OF I. P. C.- Supreme Court's Leading Case Laws

35. MOTOR VEHICLE ACT- Supreme Court's Leading Case Laws

36. CONDITION OF SERVICE- SERVICE MATTER- Supreme Court's Leading Case Laws

37. SUSPENSION- SERVICE MATTER- Supreme Court's Leading Case Laws

38. Reservation in SC, ST, OBC- Service Matter- Supreme Court's Leading Case Laws

39. NARCOTIC DRUGS AND PSYCHOTROPIC SUBSTANCES (NDPS) ACT - Supreme Court of India's Latest Leading Case Laws

40. SEC 302 IPC - Supreme Court of India's Latest Leading Case Laws

41. PROTECTION OF CHILDREN FROM SEXUAL OFFENCES ACT (POCSO) - Supreme Court of India's Latest Leading Case Laws

42. PMLA ACT BAIL MATTERS - Supreme Court of India's Leading Case Laws

43. SEC 376 BAIL MATTERS - Supreme Court of India's Leading Case Laws

44. SEC 302 BAIL MATTERS - Supreme Court of India's Leading Case Laws

45. POCSO ACT BAIL MATTERS - Supreme Court of India's Leading Case Laws

46. JUVENILE JUSTICE ACT- Supreme Court of India's Leading Case Laws

47. TRANSFER OF PROPERTY ACT- Supreme Court of India's Leading Case Laws

48. PROFESSIONAL ETHICS OF ADVOCATES- AOR EXAM- SUPREME COURT'S LEADING CASE LAWS

49. WHITE COLLAR CRIME- SUPREME COURT'S LEADING CASE LAWS

50. SEC 302 BAIL MATTERS- SUPREME COURT'S LEADING CASE LAWS

51. SEC 7 IBC 2016 - SUPREME COURT'S LATEST LEADING CASE LAW

52. ADVERSE POSSESSION IN PROPERTY MATTER - SUPREME COURT'S LATEST LEADING CASE LAWS.

53. ARMED FORCE TRIBUNAL ACT- SUPREME COURT'S LATEST LEADING CASE LAWs

54. ESSENTIAL COMMODITIES ACT 1955- SUPREME COURT'S LATEST LEADING CAS LAWS

55. 'FOOD SAFETY AND STANDARD ACT 2006' - SUPREME COURT AND HIGH COURT's LEADING CASE LAWS

Adv Jayprakash Somani's Online Courses

Download our app to get access to our Free Videos, Free Bare Acts, Free Study Material in Legal as well as International Business Regime.

Android App Link ;-https://clpandrea.page.link/cmSm

Ios APp Link :-https://apps.apple.com/us/app/classplus/id1324522260

Login with org code ;- (qywzji)

Web Link ;-https://qywzji.courses.store/

Download App on Google play store - Type

<u>Jayprakash Somani SupremeCourt</u>

Legal Courses :

1. SLP- Bail Matters- Drafting & Successful Arguing in the Supreme Court.

Description - This Course is helpful to Advocates, Litigants, Law Officers, Law Students, Law Schools, Individual. Course contains 8 Videos + Study Material+ PDF Books. Access to this course is for Two Years. Expected duration of this course is one month only.

Topics : 1. SLP- Bail Matters- Drafting & Successful Arguing in the Supreme Court, **2.** Types of bails, **3.** Laws related to bail matters, **4.** How to read Impugned Order of High Court & frame substantial question of laws, **5.** How to draft excellent SLP, **6.** Searching of citations/ case laws, **7.** How to argue in admission hearings, **8.** How argue in after notice hearing.

Speaker: Jayprakash Bansilal Somani, MBA (Foreign Trade), LL. B. Advocate, Supreme Court of India & IP www.jayprakashsomani.com Call: P. A. 9322188701

2. SLP- Succession Matters- Drafting & Successful Arguing in the Supreme Court.

Description - This Course is helpful to Advocates, Litigants, Law Officers, Law Students, Law Schools, Individual. Course contains 9 Videos + Study Material+ PDF Books. Access to this course is for Two Years. Expected duration of this course is one month only.

Topics :1. SLP- Succession Matters- Drafting & Successful Arguing in the Supreme Court, **2.** Information about Succession Matters, **3.** Laws related to Succession Matters, **4.** How to read Impugned Order of High Court to frame substantial questions of law, **5.** How to draft excellent synopsis & list of date, **6.** Drafting of SLP of Succession Matter, **7.** Searching of citations/ case laws, **8.** How to prepare notes & then argue in admission hearings, **9.** How to prepare notes & then argue in after notice final hearing.

Speaker: Jayprakash Bansilal Somani, MBA (Foreign Trade), LL. B. Advocate, Supreme Court of India & IP www.jayprakashsomani.com Call: P. A. 9322188701

3. Legal Vocabulary & its practice pattern to Argue in High Court and Supreme Court / Improve Your Legal English

Description - This Course is helpful to Advocates, Litigants, Law Officers, Law Students, Law Schools, Individual. Course contains 11 Videos + Study Material+ PDF Books. Access to this course is for Two Years. Expected duration of this course is three month only.

Topics : 1. Legal Vocabulary & its practice pattern to Argue in High Court and Supreme Court / Improve Your Legal English, **2.** 1000 legal verbs with its three forms, **3.** Twelve Tenses with its running practice, **4.** One Pdf book on legal vocabulary & its practice pattern with Latin Terms, **5.** Second Pdf book on legal vocabulary & its practice pattern with Latin Terms, **6.** Some Videos of CJI Dr. Dhananjay Chandrachud for the practice of good legal English, **7.** Some Video/Audio Lectures of Legend Nani Palkhivala for standard perfect legal English & flow of Speech, **8.** Some Videos of renowned Sr. Advocates from Mumbai for flow, legal vocabulary & their struggle in legal journey, **9.** Some Videos of Sr. Advocates of the Supreme Court for flow & legal vocabulary, **10.** Some Videos of foreign persons to improve Professional English & thinking process in English, **11.**

Some important legal doctrines with case laws.

Speaker: Jayprakash Bansilal Somani, MBA (Foreign Trade), LL. B. Advocate, Supreme Court of India & IP www.jayprakashsomani.com Call: P. A. 9322188701.

4. SLP- Property Matters - Drafting and Successful Arguing in the Supreme Court.

Description - This Course is helpful to Advocates, Litigants, Law Officers, Law Students, Law Schools 8 Individual. Course contains 9 Videos + Study Material+ PDF Books. Access to this course is for Two Years. Expected duration of this course is one month only.

Topics : 1. SLP- Property Matters - Drafting and Successful Arguing in the Supreme Court, **2.** Types of Property Matters, **3.** Laws related to Property Matters, **4.** How to read Impugned Order of High Court to guide client & frame substantial question of laws, **5.** How to draft Synopsis & List of Dates in Property Matter, **6.** How to draft excellent SLP of Property Matter, **7.** Searching of citations/ case laws with specific paras, **8.** How to argue confidently in admission hearings, **9.** How argue confidently in after notice & final hearings.

Speaker: Jayprakash Bansilal Somani, MBA (Foreign Trade), LL. B. Advocate, Supreme Court of India & IP www.jayprakashsomani.com Call: P. A. 9322188701.

International Business Courses -

1. Agri Products Exports - Scope from India.

Description - This Course is helpful to Agriculturalists, Entrepreneurs, Exporters, Importers, Students. Course contains 12 Videos + Study Material+ PDF Books. Access to this course is for Two Years. Expected duration of this course is one month only.

Topics : 1- Agri Products Exports - Scope from India, **2.** Agri Export's share in India's total export, **3.** Agri Export Promotional Council's Support, **4.** Top 10 Agri export countries, **5.** Top 10 Agri export product, **6.** India's share in World's Agri Exports, **7.** Onion Exports from India, **8.** Rice Exports from India, **9.** Mango Exports from India, **10.** Fresh Vegetable Exports, **11.** Fresh Fruits Exports, **12.** Export of Agri Allied Products.

Speaker: Jayprakash Bansilal Somani, MBA (Foreign Trade), LL. B. Advocate, Supreme Court of India & IP www.jayprakashsomani.com Call: P. A. 9322188701.

2. Textile Exports - Scope from India.

Description - This Course is helpful to Textile Business Houses, Entrepreneurs, Exporters, Importers, Students. Course contains 14 Videos + Study Material+ PDF Books. Access to this course is for Two Years. Expected duration of this course is one month only.

Topics : 1- Textile Exports - Scope from India, **2.** Textile Export's share in India's total exports, **3.** Support of Textile Export Promotional Council, **4.** Top 10 Countries in Textile Exports, **5.** Top 10 Products in Textile Exports, **6.** Export of Readymade Garments, **7.** Export of Man-made Textiles, **8.** Export of Handloom Products, **9.** Export of Wool & Woollen Textiles, **10.** Export of Silk, **11.** Exports of Handicrafts & Carpets, **12.** Exports of Coir & Coir Manufacturers, **13.** Exports of Jute,14. India's share in World's total textile expor.

Speaker: Jayprakash Bansilal Somani, MBA (Foreign Trade), LL. B. Advocate, Supreme Court of India & IP www.jayprakashsomani.com Call: P. A. 9322188701.

3. Export Import Procedure -Perfect Documentation & It's Management.

Description -This Course is helpful to Business Men, Service Providers, Entrepreneurs, Exporters, Importers, Students. Course contains 13 Videos + Study Material+ PDF Books. Access to this course is for Two Years. Expected duration of this course is three months only.

Topics : 1. Export Import Procedure, Perfect Documentation & Its management, **2.** Company Formation, **3.** Opening of Bank Account in AD Bank, **4.** Export Procedure points, **5.** Import Procedure Points, **6.** Taking Import Export Code, **7.** Taking RCMC number, **8.** Registration at Port when necessary, **9.** Quality Inspection Certificate of Goods, **10.** CHA & its roll, **11.** Custom Formalities, **12.** Export Documents such as Invoice, Bill of Lading, Insurance Certificate, Quality Inspection Certificate & others, **13.** Excellent Management of Export & Imports Documents.

Speaker: Jayprakash Bansilal Somani, MBA (Foreign Trade), LL. B. Advocate, Supreme Court of India & IP www.jayprakashsomani.com Call: P. A. 9322188701.

4. Jewellery Exports -Scope from India

Description - You can understand world wide scope for Jems & Jewellery in multidimensional ways. 14 videos of this course will create positive spark among you to enter into the Exports & Imports of Gems & Jewellery and other products. Chance to ask your query to Somani Sir every week.

Topics :1. Jewellery Exports - Scope from India, **2.** Jewellery Export's share in India's total exports, **3.** Support of Jems & Jewellery Export Promotional Council, **4.** Top 10 Countries in Jewellery Exports, **5.** Top 10 Products in Jewellery Exports, **6.** Export of Cut & Polished Diamonds, **7.** Export of Gold Jewellery, **8.** Export of Plain Gold Jewellery, **9.** Export of Studded Gold Jewellery, **10.** Export of Silver Jewellery, **11.** Exports of Platinum Jewellery, **12.** Exports of Imitation Jewellery, **13.** Exports of Articles of Gold, Silver & others, **14.** India's share in World's total Jewellery export.

Speaker: Jayprakash Bansilal Somani, MBA (Foreign Trade), LL. B. Advocate, Supreme Court of India & IP www.jayprakashsomani.com Call: P. A. 9322188701.

5. Export Import Finance Management with LC, ECGC & Venture Capital.

Description -You can understand A to Z about International Finance with LC, ECGC & Venture Capital in simple language & with illustrations. 11 videos of this course will create positive spark among you regarding International Finance Management with practical tips. Chance to ask your query to Somani Sir every week.

Topics : 1. Export Import Finance Management with LC, ECGC & Venture Capital, **2.** Which is good & excellent source of finance, **3.** Banking Finance, **4.** List of Banks which provides finance for International Business, **5.** How to start business in Less or Zero Capital, **6.** Letter of Credit, **7.** Types of LCs **8.** Scrutiny of L/C, **9.** ECGC Policy, **10.** Venture Capital Finance., **11.** Ideal formula of Investment & continues growth.

Speaker: Jayprakash Bansilal Somani, MBA (Foreign Trade), LL. B. Advocate, Supreme Court of India & IP www.jayprakashsomani.com Call: P. A. 9322188701.

6. Shipping & Logistics in International Business with live links of Ports, ICDs, CHAs etc.

Description - This Course is helpful to any Businessman, Professionals, Entrepreneurs, Exporters, Importers, CHAs, & Students.

Course contains following 10 Videos + Study Material+ PDF Books. Access to this course is for Two Years. Expected duration of this course is three months only.

Topics : 1. Shipping & Logistics in International Business with live links of Ports, ICDs, CHAs etc, **2.** Roll of CHA in Shipping & Logistics of International Business, **3.** How to find good & genuine CHA, **4.** Courier/

post service for small parcel, **5.** India's important Ports & ICDs with live links, **6.** How & what to study Ports/ ICDs websites, **7.** Art to reduce charges of Shipping & logistics, **8.** Information about some Top International Ports with live links, **9.** Roll of Customs in Exports & Imports,**10.** How to become CHA .

Speaker: Jayprakash Bansilal Somani, MBA (Foreign Trade), LL. B. Advocate, Supreme Court of India & IP www.jayprakashsomani.com Call: P. A. 9322188701.

7. International Business Marketing Part 1: Finding Potential & Genuine Buyers for Exports and Suppliers for Imports.

Description -You can understand Seven Excellent ways to Find Potential & Genuine Buyers for Exports and Suppliers for Imports with illustrations. 11 videos of this course will create positive spark among you regarding International Business Marketing with practical tips. Chance to ask your query to Somani Sir every week.

Topics : 1. International Business Marketing Part 1: Finding Potential & Genuine Buyers for Exports and Suppliers for Imports,**2.** Seven Excellent Ways to find Potential Buyers for Exports, **3.** Top 20 B to B Websites in the World, **4.** Searching Potential Buyers from B to B Sites. Is this safe & good way to search potential buyers, **5.** Searching Potential Buyers through Export Promotional Councils & Its Magazines, **6.** Searching Potential Buyers with help from Embassies, **7.** Searching Potential Buyers through Chamber of Commerce at global level, **8.** Searching Potential Buyers from International Trade Fairs & Exhibitions, **9.** Searching Potential Buyers through your friends & relatives or any Indian Person in focus countries, **10.** How to find focus countries for your products or services, **11.** Taking references from establish buyer/seller.

Speaker: Jayprakash Bansilal Somani, MBA (Foreign Trade), LL. B. Advocate, Supreme Court of India & IP www.jayprakashsomani.com Call: P. A. 9322188701.

8. International Business Marketing Part 2: Communication Skill to take repeated orders from Potential Buyers

Description - You can learn Perfect Communication Skills to initiate International Trade with foreign buyers and art to take repeated orders from these Potential Buyers with illustrations. 11 videos of this course will create positive spark among you to reach upto One Star Exporter Level rapidly and subsequent journey to reach upto Five Star Export House. Chance to ask your query to Somani Sir every week.

Topics :1. International Business Marketing Part 2: Communication Skill to take repeated orders from Potential Buyers,**2.** Preparation of Impressive Company Profile, **3.** Excellent Product CatLog for International Market, **4.** Phone Calls with maintaining dignity of ourself & our country, **5.** Sending emails, **6.** Sending what's app messages, **7.** Technique of repeated follow up, **8.** Art of taking 100% advance payments, **9.** Before giving credit facility how to look credibility of potential buyers or suppliers, **10.** Art of earning good profit of margin, **11.** Art of managing international clients.

Speaker: Jayprakash Bansilal Somani, MBA (Foreign Trade), LL. B. Advocate, Supreme Court of India & IP www.jayprakashsomani.com Call: P. A. 9322188701.

www.ingramcontent.com/pod-product-compliance
Lightning Source LLC
Chambersburg PA
CBHW041336120726
48005CB00014B/2278